"Ours is not to seek popularity for ourselves
or to impress seekers with the depth of our knowledge
but only to put the written word in their hands
and so give them a better understanding
of the world in which they live."

NB: The terms 'man' and 'mankind' used throughout this book represent the male and female collective unless specified to the contrary.

The Bridge of Awareness

A handbook for understanding life
compiled from
The Teachings of Zed

by
Jane Tinworth

World Awareness Trust

Copyright © 2011 Jane Tinworth

All rights reserved. No part of this publication may be may be reproduced, stored in a retrieval system, or transmitted in any form or by any means, electronic or mechanical, photocopying, recording or otherwise, without the prior permission of the publisher of this book, such permission in respect of short extracts will not be unreasonably withheld.

Published by the
World Awareness Trust
PO Box 95
Teignmouth
TQ14 4AY
Devon, UK
www.worldawarenesstrust.org

ISBN 978-0-9568619-0-0

Printed by Parrott Printing Torquay

INTRODUCTION

This is a book like no other. Between these pages you will find the foundations for the understanding of life itself, from the meaning of our everyday trials and tribulations to our connectedness with the universe and the oneness of all things. Set out in simple language and yet with the resonance of Truth, the words take you through a progressive and cohesive journey of spiritual discovery that makes sense of the big questions of life by placing them within a deep and yet understandable framework. Perhaps more than anything though, these teachings – for that is what they are – are carried on the wings of divine love to the present age of humankind to offer us all the gift of greater awareness, and therefore of greater choice.

Within the cycles of the universe, the beginning of each new age heralds in a shift in energy for the planet together with a set of updated understandings and codes for living. Such are these teachings. The words you read here are not mine: they came from another dimension of awareness over a period of years to a small group of friends, little by little, informing and challenging with time to digest. My particular role was to accurately record, safeguard and compile them under headings for ultimate distribution and therefore the words you read are the words that were received, free of personal opinion or interpretation.

I have now worked with these Teachings for over twenty years, endeavouring to place them at the heart of my inner and outer life and sharing them with others throughout the world by way of meetings, workshops and writings. I can truly say with the weight of experience that what you will find here is most likely to be deeply meaningful, not just as a set of ideas but as a reference and guide for the way in which you choose to live your life. It is for this reason that I prefer to classify this book as a manual, or handbook for life, unlike the kind of sacred writings that remain under the authority of a particular belief system.

Time and again throughout this book you will be faced with the challenges of self-responsibility in your every thought, word and action, but you will also discover the rewards of greater love and awareness in all that you are and all that you do. You will find that the information you need at any step of the way already exists within a part of you and can be accessed directly by you. It is therefore evident that you do not need anyone else to read the book on your behalf and then give you their conclusions. This is not to say that the words are not to be shared with others: on the contrary, it is hoped they will be studied, discussed and debated between other open-minded people inside homes, meeting places and over the Internet.

The important point to remember is that each individual will see the words from their own conditioned viewpoint at any point in time so none will be completely right or completely wrong, and that is as it should be, otherwise these teachings would face the danger of becoming yet another dogma. This is an extract of what was said on the subject:

"The teachings must be examined and choices made. Don't expect others to come to the same conclusions that you have immediately. Each person will interpret an abstract painting differently from the artist but the important thing is that it starts them thinking. When you look at our teachings, start with a blank sheet of paper: you'll find it much easier, for if you have written many thoughts before you start then you then have to justify those thoughts with the teachings. Try it the other way round - it's much easier."

This collection of words is identified as The Teachings of Zed but they are not the product of an individual but a collective, or level, of awareness. The speaker for the collective recognised the need for a label, or name, and suggested that a letter of the alphabet might be appropriate. The last letter of the English alphabet was chosen: Zed. It is right that I end this introduction with these words from it/them/him:

"The words we speak are simply words: they have no value until others perceive them, take meaning from them, and act upon them. They are not my property, they are not your property, they are part of the Universe. We ask you to protect them only to keep their purity and simplicity.

"And if you see these words with meaning and understanding, and if they feel part of you, if they start to form the structure and base of your spiritual understanding, then the needs that you decide in life will be based against those understandings."

Jane Tinworth
2011.

*"The Teachings will be simple to understand
but will take a lifetime to execute."*

Isn't it incredible that man has been on this planet for so long and yet has difficulty diagnosing his reason for being here? He rushes blindly around seeking to consolidate his worldly issues, yet spares little thought for the meaning of his existence.

Chapter One

It is good for everyone to reflect on the central issue of life, for many go from birth to death and rarely consider it and each religion differs slightly in the way that it is interpreted. Materialism, particularly in the western world, is the predominant feature of your life and you see little purpose in following a spiritual path and yet this is the reason you came so the vast majority of you live through each life completely blind to the reason you are here. Mankind is now coming to the level and time when if civilisation is to mean anything, profound questions need to be asked.

Many conclude that the reason for man's presence here is to learn from the experiences of each lifetime and in terms of learning that is correct. But there must also be an objective for such learning. That is what we mean by the central issue of life.

The path we advocate you follow in pursuit of spiritual understanding is a simple one and open to all, for it would be wrong if the way were shrouded in secrecy, complicated rituals or a reliance on other individuals. The route we suggest is dependent only on you, your efforts and your discipline because it is a unique and inward journey that leads to the higher self. There is no quick access and no religion can automatically qualify you if the life you lead is alien to it. But when you discover the gate to the higher self, you discover the gate to God – however or whatever you conceive God to be.

What is the higher self? It is the soul. It is that portion of you that never leaves you, that journeys through lifetimes with you, that never dies. It determines who you are, which parents you are born to, where you are born, the kind of mind and body you inhabit and your direction in life. Over the many lifetimes you share, the higher self is your common link to the universe and to God. Through this link you may access not only the solutions to your problems and the awareness of who you truly are, but the knowledge and experience of life itself.

Always remember that with the higher self you are part of God: that a portion within you is within the heart of God at all times. So it may appear that you have a strange anomaly arising, because even though it is separate it is still part of the whole, not divorced from universal power, not on its own in the wilderness, but surrounded by total universal love.

In the past millennia, man has sought such answers outside himself and within organisations, the majority of which have tended merely to reflect the aspirations of the seekers in looking at themselves in relation to the planet and its past. Man still continuously strives to relate his higher self to his body and the planet when in reality he should be looking within to his higher self and the universe, to understand the true purpose of life. This failing on Earth of only looking at itself in isolation must change. The new millennium has to be a universal concept.

Imagine an ant: its world is its nest and all it can see. You are the same on this planet for you strive to relate only to what you see and not in reality to what exists. So you seek thoughts and feelings of a spiritual nature only within the parameters of your visual experience. Do not relate only to the planet for it is just a tiny fraction of an immense universe and there are planets and forms beyond anything you can see or envisage; worlds of incredible love beyond your comprehension. You spend your resources trying to protect little areas of land on your planet instead of grouping together your scientific knowledge throughout the world in an endeavour to understand the mysticism of the universe.

Science, as you know it on Earth, is the part of mysticism that can be measured. For 3,000 years energy has been written about by great teachers and in time science will discover how the measurement of spiritual energy may be achieved. In the meantime it is not our intention to divulge the secrets of the universe, for such would destroy the karma of the world, but to correct the wrong opinion that spiritual energy is related to light waves. If that were the case, you would be able to see and measure it. The fact that you cannot does not mean that it does not exist.

>To explain further we give you four words:
>1. Universal
>2. Cosmic
>3. Dynamic
>4. Energy
>
>By 'universal' we mean available *everywhere*, omnipresent.
>By 'cosmic' we mean it *transcends time and space*.
>By 'dynamic' we mean it *motivates*, can be used, it is alive.
>By 'energy' we mean a *spiritual force*.

Light travels at 186,000 miles per second and science currently assumes that this is the fastest means of travel within the universe. Light is composed of waves and particles that are susceptible to the force of gravity. Within the terms of science as you know it, that is correct. However, man's direct link to spiritual energy is not light but *thought,* for thought is *instantaneous.*

Cosmic energy is the creative force of the universe; it was there before its conception and not as a consequence. It is instantaneous throughout the universe; it knows no time, no distance. Because thought is directly linked to the cosmic force, the energy in terms of what you think lives forever. The concept may be mind-blowing, but if thought transcends time and space then its consequences are *limitless.*

The energy is universal and constant. It can be used for different purposes. The way it is motivated is by thought, and the greater the spiritual awareness of the individual, the greater their access to the energy. So the thoughts of a healer, for example, will carry energy motivated by thoughts of love and compassion and the recipient of the energy will then interpret it as they wish for healing themselves.

Be aware therefore that thought is a powerful instrument, a tool that can be used for good or ill. Consider then the importance of being aware of your thoughts at every moment, for you truly are masters of your own destiny.

The danger with human beings is in achieving purity of thought at all times, for the unkind thoughts you have throughout the day not only hurt others but yourself. It is therefore important to train the mind to have good thoughts. The first stage in this training is to be critical of your own thoughts, to become aware of unkind or unhelpful thoughts. The second stage is to be tolerant of the thoughts of others. If you can learn to return unkind thoughts with kindness and love then it neutralises the animosity they bring. It is like throwing an angry stone into a pond and large ripples go outwards, but with good thoughts you pour oil on the water and the ripples have less effect. If you apply these basic principles then you will be on the right road.

All the great teachers and all the great theologies through history have advocated this but few have achieved it. It is a fact that spiritual ways are not complicated or difficult to understand but they are very hard to practise.

As you develop the power of thought and learn about its consequences, so your mind becomes more spiritually aware. And as we have said, the more spiritually aware you become, the greater energy your thought will carry. Then from the resulting increase in awareness comes the ability to control your thought and use it in a better way. The third and essential step in this process is *meditation*, for it is the key that unlocks the door to your higher self.

Everything reacts to thought; human beings, plant and animal life and the planet itself. And every thought, every movement, makes its impression on the universe. It therefore follows that the energy created by collective thought has great impact, so groups who gather to pray or meditate together attune their thoughts collectively to a spiritual direction and thus generate a powerful energy of love. But your personal path can only be achieved through looking inwards.

When you look around, you see life as it is, as the Creator made it, so what you think about is what you see. This is so for any kind of environment you occupy, whether at work, at home or elsewhere, for what you see is what you think about. But when you meditate you still the mind and see what is within and so raise your awareness. How else can you find your higher self except within yourself, for the spiritual staircase is within, not outside?

But all the meditating in the world is of no use unless you practise what you learn from it.

Each individual needs to develop meditation in their own way for each one is different in how they approach themselves. There are, however, some basic points relevant to all methods. One of these is how to distinguish between what is the mind and what is the higher self, for the mind is of this lifetime only and conditioned by the thoughts of others from the moment of birth.

The mind is a fickle thing, it jumps and starts and imagines falsely, and until you can settle the mind, until you can nullify its effects, you cannot even find the staircase. To achieve this requires *dedication* and *discipline* because the mind has been programmed to look outward, to be active, and is therefore unwilling to yield its control. Just as an unruly child needs firm but loving guidance for its own good and that of society, so the mind needs clear parameters in which to operate. Then, with steady practice, the surface of the water becomes still and it is easier to differentiate between the conditioned thoughts of the mind and intuitive guidance from within.

The world today could learn a lot from our teachings on the benefits of meditation for as we have said, this is the only key to a person's inner awareness, to their higher self. Unfortunately, few take the subject seriously for they fail to understand its real potential. It is important to understand that apart from meditation, unity with the higher self is possible only in three other states:

1. the child in the womb
2. at certain times in deep sleep, and
3. in the full trance state of mediumship.

Of these alternatives, you clearly cannot return to your mother's womb or rely upon the occasional and unpredictable times when in sleep the mind opens to allow the wisdom of the higher self to emerge. And the full-trance state is available only to those with certain inborn psychic abilities. But as we have said, the pathway is open to all and therefore the only sure and direct route is through meditation.

These are not new revelations, they have been known for thousands of years, yet man ignores them and ridicules them, thus cutting himself off from higher spiritual knowledge. Now is the time to redress this imbalance and seize the opportunity for a new awareness that for thousands of years has lain dormant and not been used to its fullest potential.

We have talked to you of energy, of thought, of awareness, and now we have talked of the doorway to it all. From these primitive and basic understandings, mankind has the opportunity to understand the universe in its entirety. This is why continual reference is made to the need for meditation. And here is the big one: that the time will come when people will break from the complexities of the material world and seek within themselves the power to heal their own ailments and have complete unity with themselves in a spiritual sense, thus fulfilling the objective of their presence on Earth.

The path will not always be smooth, for there are those who will see this as a challenge to the status and wealth they have acquired through teaching complicated beliefs in which the poor seeker can only find salvation in either health or religion through complex procedures involving more intelligent beings on the planet. In reality, what we are now proposing is that they have all the answers they need within themselves at no cost to themselves or anyone else except discipline, good thinking and good living. It's so simple!

Let us now consider the role of meditation in relation to religious teachings.

Nearly always, a person's particular religious belief is based on their birthplace. In England you are likely to be born a Christian, in India a Hindu, in Pakistan a Muslim, and so on throughout the world. Your religion is the religion of the country you were born into or the religion of your parents, which in turn was probably based on the circumstances of their birth. The essential question to consider here is whether inner awareness is contradictory to religious beliefs. The answer is that of course it is not, for it is one and the same, but unfortunately many do not see this.

The trouble is that religious beliefs many hundreds of years old have good concepts but fail to build on them. For example, how many modern Christians try to relate their present knowledge to the teachings of Christ? No religion should be static in its interpretation and that is why many religions of the world are dying. For what is seen as truth is only an assessment of the knowledge we have available at that time. So, as our knowledge expands, so our interpretation of the truth changes. That does not alter our fundamental beliefs, but only our interpretation of them. In other words, as an example, in taking the teachings of Jesus as a basic code for living, you have to relate them to what they mean today and not what they meant two thousand years ago.

Many hold on to the dogmas and doctrines of their religions and thereby mask themselves from the reality of those teachings as they apply today. For however you see God, the progress of yourself within that master plan is the most significant issue. You should see teachings in relation to how they can improve yourself and your spiritual awareness and how you live, and not as many do, in blind obedience to doctrines and rituals that many use for political and economic power. We must return again to the simple belief that each of us is as important as the other in the eyes of God and we must move towards a greater understanding of ourselves and a greater understanding of our role in the society in which we live. The key to such awareness lies within. The roadway to that goal is meditation.

So the two important points to be aware of are these: you as an individual and your relationship to God.

There has been, through religious practices, a tendency to abrogate individual responsibility in the name of religion. One has seen throughout history, for example, how religious leaders on opposing sides each bless their soldiers before battle. Where does the individual's role in his relation to his Creator fit into that? These are the questions that need to be answered now, in the modern context, for God is Universal Love: how then can you kill in His name? So you see what we mean by your conduct in the eyes of your God and how that relates to your personal responsibility and karma.

Unquestioning acceptance of any teaching cannot be healthy or proper for you were not put on this planet to practise blind faith but to seek the Truth. The motivation for this is *love*. Start with yourself and then you can move to others. In this way you can truly move closer to God. In simple terms, you love yourself so that you can love others, and by so doing you join Universal Love.

It is funny, isn't it, how people see doing good things for themselves as wrong. They would perhaps just frown on someone if they never washed, but would throw up their hands in horror at the thought of loving themselves. We see no conflict of interest, nothing wrong in this, for there is a world of difference between loving yourself and being selfish. They are opposite ends of the scale, not the same side.

In your moments of loneliness, remember you are all part of God.

The High Street of Life

Many of you walk the High Street of Life. On each side of you, you see the big shops and stores brightly lit in the grey of your lives: the shops of temptation, the shops of materialism, the main store of greed; they are important in your lives, you are envious of those that walk into those stores to fill their arms with the material things of life. But we say to you, walk past these shops, look not to right or left, look instead for the little street on the side where the sun is breaking through the grey and against the wall the name of this street shines, 'Love and Awareness'.

Turn into that little side street and as you do so, be not foiled by the large churches that appear to block its entrances, but walk on, and leading off from there you will see the little bookshop with just simply 'Love' written across the top. You will have to bend to enter and the doorway will be old for it has been there since man was conceived. But open the door and walk in, and there on the wall will be our teachings, there in quietness of meditation on your own you can consider the words.

Then when you return to the main street, the sun will follow you and you will walk down the middle of that street lit by the sun's rays of Universal Love. And from the grey surrounding you others will wish to join that light for it will shine brighter than the fluorescent lights of the shops around.

There will always be those who will try to stop you for they cannot see the relevance of the little side street you walked to acquire that knowledge. Meet their arguments with love and compassion and understanding.

—

On the blackboard of life in indelible chalk
your mind writes its choices.
Ultimately your higher self has to account for those choices.
Such is the way of karma. Such is the way of Universal Law.

Chapter Two

The wisdom you look for lies within you. Your inner wisdom is all you need, for within it lies not only the solutions to your problems but to all the secrets of the universe. But like a child when it first sees a book, it cannot understand the truth for first it must learn to read: only then does it unlock the door to inner wisdom. Such is meditation. By learning to meditate you learn to read your inner self, then as your progress becomes more advanced, so you are able to discern what is inner wisdom and what is imagination because with a trained mind, true clarity is apparent.

Seek spiritual awareness in a clear and open way, for that is the true way to the higher self. Excitement distorts the path. So though you may experience many wonders, learn to look upon them with detachment. This is particularly important for those with a psychic ability who may easily become mesmerised by the visual sensations they encounter as they climb the tree of meditation.

Psychic experience can be interpreted by different people in different ways and many confuse it with normal inner visualisation, which employs the imagination of the mind. The definition of 'psychic' is therefore important: *it is an experience beyond the mind.* So you see the need for achieving clarity of inner wisdom, for without it you are unable to differentiate between the two.

Only when you have a higher inner awareness can you experience psychic phenomena; it is a consequence of higher awareness but not an essential part of it. Some find the road easy and don't have to work at it and others have great difficulty and never achieve it. But always remember the goal is not psychic phenomena but your higher self. Those who seek to find solutions only in psychic terms have surely taken the wrong road for do they see it as their only reason for existence? If so, then they are heading for spiritual disaster because they will become entangled in the branches of psychic sensationalism which will prevent them climbing higher. We say again that psychic experience is not a prerequisite to higher inner awareness, but only a consequence of it. The only advantage of looking along the branches is that it gives you an incentive to climb.

Seeking union with the higher self at the top of the tree is the objective. In this way you gain access to all knowledge.

At its creation the higher self is part of Ultimate Knowledge: One. Why then should it start its journey if it already has ultimate knowledge? Why should it need experience? Focus on 'awareness' and you will come to understand more.

The higher self has access to all knowledge. What it lacks is the awareness of that knowledge. As it develops, so its access increases. Through experience - the gateway to awareness - the higher self increases its access to all knowledge. It therefore follows that the higher self moves through levels, or dimensions, of awareness before its journey is complete.

A simple analogy of this is of a fruit that falls from a tree: as it lies on the ground it is only aware of itself as a separate entity, a seed within an outer coat. Then through the experience of growth it becomes more aware of itself until finally it reaches its full potential and awareness as the tree itself. The knowledge of that potential was within the seed from the beginning but only with experience could the fruit realise its true nature.

The higher self therefore incarnates in order to gain experience from which it may raise its awareness of itself. The kinds of experiences it encounters are determined within the law of karma by its need for awareness.

Because of man's reluctance to accept certain laws that he finds distasteful, he assumes that things within the spiritual realms are haphazard, but this is not so. Laws govern all things throughout the universe. Man observes certain fundamental laws of physics, so why should higher understandings be any different? The fact that man has no knowledge of them does not mean they do not exist. Nothing can exist outside universal laws, for within the total accumulations of all laws is Ultimate Knowledge.

Karma is the universal law of cause and effect, of personal and collective responsibility for every thought and action. In the past this has often been seen as a law of judgement and punishment for wrongdoing but this is far from the truth, for karma is a process of expanding awareness which, like all universal laws, is motivated only by love.

Through transitional thought the time is decided for the implementation of karmic law for each individual: that is the prerogative of the higher self within the law of karma. The definition of transitional thought is the evaluation of actions between two points of time: what is important now is dependent on what happened in the past and what will happen in the future. We relate it like this to you but from our point of view it is timeless. This information is all new and needs to be carefully considered and understood. Perhaps though, the relevance of training your mind and thought is now becoming more apparent.

When the higher self selects the body it requires for an incarnation, it also selects the mind, for both are physical tools of experience. What then stops the mind from aspiring to the wishes of the higher self?

The mind can be said to be the doorway to the higher self. Your higher self chooses the mind best suited for the experiences it needs but the mind then has choice of its own. If this were not so then the mind would be a mere puppet of the higher self and there would be little point in existence on Earth. Due to the mind's lack of awareness of its higher self, its training is within the everyday world in which it lives and nearly always this is based against its three inherent negative components: greed, anger and ignorance. The ancients said that within these three were contained all the negative aspects of the mind.

Do you now see how that opens the pathway to wider understanding? Do not look at the mind in isolation, for it has become a victim of choice and by the acquiring of negative qualities has shut the door on the love and wisdom from within. But by overcoming ignorance, you overcome greed and anger, for as you become aware so you open the door. Such creates the experience of life.

Consider the young mind: the more spiritually protected and the less materialistic a child's upbringing is, the more their door stands ajar for contrary to belief, at birth the door was wide open. But as the person grows the mind is fed with intellect. Then because of the knowledge they have encountered they seek an eye-level lock but one is not to be found, for the lock is lower down the door. Because of their ego, a consequence of their intellectual superiority, they won't look lower down the door, saying no lock exists and so they cannot open the door. However, to the young child standing by the side of these intellectually supreme beings, the child whose mind has not been tarnished by the material world, he looks up and sees the lock clearly for it is above him. He is not yet old enough to put the key in the lock and he can just look through and see the keyhole. Then society turns him around and he looks the other way and he grows in intellect and material gain. Eventually he remembers and turns around to look for the lock, but by that time he has grown and once more the lock is below him and he does not see it.

The ancients understood this and that is why in many religions of the world, young children were taken from their homely environment into a sacred place to ensure that they always looked for the keyhole. But sadly, religious leaders, to justify their ego and financial ambitions, piled images in front of the doorway to obscure the child's vision. Then as he grew, all he could see was the visual image of a god his religion *said* existed, when behind the door all the time, his higher self was crying out in need for help and experience.

It is also necessary to take into account the role of karma in relation to the door, for many obstruct it with the material pathway. Consider carefully the need to clear the rubbish from the door, for these are the riches you accumulate in life. Be aware that the door is very simply opened and if the locks and hinges are stiff, then the oilcan of love will soon free them and the key of awareness will open it.

What of those who do not seek? Their door is closed and the hinges grow rusty. And as the hinges grow rusty so the door is harder to open. Then if their door remains closed they will have no alternative but to come again with a new door in a new lifetime, hoping that their mind will become more aware and open the door more fully for them. So you see the wisdom of those that meditate wisely, opening and shutting their door and ensuring the free movement of the hinges.

Always there is choice. The hard thing to accept is that the greater the intellect, the harder the choice becomes, for intellect breeds ego.

Take a mountain stream as an example. At its source the water is pure and clear and as it flows down we see it as the stream of life. The further it flows the more it grows in magnitude and speed. From its birth as a small stream to the adult as a river, this now River of Life has on its left bank many that walk in the direction of the current, for the left bank is the bank of *ego*. Those with less understanding carry on walking towards the mouth of the river but if they were to look to the right they would see the bridges of spiritual awareness and cross to the bank of *love*. The problem is that on that side they would be hidden from the view of all those that surround them, for here on the left bank of ego many follow them and they have great power, great prestige and riches: people shout their names and call them 'great ones'. But the truly great ones are they that walk to the right bank where no riches, no materialism, no recognition except that of shared love exists. It is not an easy pathway to take for it is contrary to all they have learned, but it is not a long bridge either. The problem is that until they reach the right bank they are obscured from their spiritual progress.

Many of those that lead will have little motivation to cross: they even question the whole concept of spiritual awareness. But those who seek will become disillusioned with what they see for the leaders are so bound up with their egos that they don't even recognise that a bridge exists. Fortunately, seekers will soon discover the hollowness of the reasoning of these ego-hunters and will look for a deeper meaning in their lives. Often they are motivated initially by finding a way out of their suffering but soon they learn that this was nothing - merely a lesson in direction to their real awareness. Then in learning from their problems they see the true pathway over the bridge.

Many abrogate their responsibility of choice by saying that evil deeds are part of the learning of the higher self. But when the universe, of which the higher self is part, consists of the universal love energy, how could it be motivated to evil? Do you see now the difficulty in understanding the difference between the choice of the mind and the needs of the higher self? These are very central questions that need to be considered by the whole movement throughout the world.

Highly evolved souls have come to the earthplane to experience and they have within them great energy and great knowledge. Do you think the universe and universal love would be the motivating force for them to be responsible for millions of deaths? Such would make a mockery of the learning experience of love. So do not try to explain evil deeds as the motivation of the higher self needing to learn by such wrong experiences.

The mind has choice at all levels. Let us assume, for example, that a high level entity, incarnating to raise its awareness, has a mind that becomes motivated by greed. It did not come for the object of greed but that is what the mind has chosen and as a consequence of that it would have to return to repeat the exercise and also undo the harm it has done. That does not relate to its level except to show that it has not developed its full awareness. Because it has a high level of awareness does not absolve it from the responsibility of the law of karma on the earthplane. And of course, when the higher self has reached any particular level of awareness it cannot become less aware than it was before - only *more accountable* for the choices of the mind. It is therefore important to understand that highly evolved souls do not necessarily lead good lives.

What is it that attracts followers to a person? It is their spiritual power. Who was one of the most powerful men of the twentieth century? Adolf Hitler. Hitler attracted millions to him because he was a highly evolved being but he used that power in pursuit of ego and as a result thousands and thousands followed him, resulting in the most terrible suffering and group karma. Compare this to the choices of another highly evolved soul of the same era, Mahatma Gandhi. Even Jesus had choice. What would have happened if He had given in to self?

Have you done bad things in past lives and in this incarnation? Of course! It is self. But you have to experience the bad to appreciate the good for they are two sides of the same coin.

We have touched on some important aspects here for, as we have said, rather than assume that the mind operates at random, understand that in general it moves negatively as a consequence of those three aspects: anger, greed and ignorance.

Consider the value placed on such a precious commodity as a simple glass of water. Would you not agree it is the nutrient of life? A society that values gold and silver but ignores the very nutrient of life simply because you have been blessed with so much of it, does that not reflect the attitude of society as a whole? The law of supply and demand is a man-made law. A person who had all the gold and silver in the world but was lying parched in the desert, would he not give it all for a glass of water? Man needs to think about all he holds dear around him, to reappraise his values in life. Is it not obvious that something is wrong when one half of the planet conceals the gems and gold and silver so the world cannot see them whilst the other half needs the most precious commodity of all? Until man rethinks his values of the real worth around him, how can he address the central question of what is within him? It is not a chicken-and-egg situation, for by wise living, by understanding the real values of all around him, he then opens the doors to the true riches within him.

Why cannot mankind see the planet as a garden that could provide food for all? Why must they fence portions of it off to exclude poorer countries from enjoying the benefits it provides? Until these central questions are resolved, how can you have a peaceful world, a world that was intended to develop spiritual awareness of all on it when with every step you take you alienate your own environment? You seek to control the population but for the wrong reasons; so that half the world can go on enjoying the wealth while the other half remains poor. If the wealthier parts were honest with themselves, they would admit that they see the third world countries' expansion as simply costing them more. That is not to say that consideration does not need to be made to population control, but this should be against the planet's ability to provide food and not against monetary considerations.

How many of you in this country today consider your *real* needs - the food you eat and the water you drink? How much more important you consider it to be to have a metal box with four wheels that can hurtle you around the planet at enormous speeds, polluting the atmosphere and burning valuable resources. How many of you when you drive, seriously consider whether you need to go as fast as you do, for when you get to the other end, do you not then sit down, take some refreshment and boast how short a time the journey took you? This serves merely as a small example of the wrong values of a society that has lost its way, a society that uses technology in the wrong way - not to feed the hungry, but to further its material ambitions.

The time will come in the future as a consequence of man's greed that an economic crisis and a world-wide shortage of food will force man to look at the pathway he is walking. Because of the involvement and the motivation of religious and holy men throughout the world, they will bring little comfort to the population at this critical point. Our writings will be the key to their awareness but they will have the choice: to accept or reject them. We cannot force people to believe these words but when the hungry man looks for food and sees the loaf of bread on the table, then he reaches for it. So it will be spiritually with our teachings. *We* do not create the hunger, the greed, the selfishness, the wilful destruction of this beautiful planet; *we* do not let millions of you starve while others grow fat; *we* do not cut down your trees and burn your forests; *we* do not make you kill each other for gain and if many of your religious leaders say that this is our justice on man then they abrogate, by so doing, their own responsibility for not making man aware of what they do to each other.

Never in your history on this planet have you been so capable of destroying your own environment and that of all those who share the planet with you - and yet still you have choice. And as we endeavour to raise the conscience of the world to what everybody does, still the motivation is greed. Mankind has never had an opportunity like he has now where the resources of the world could be harnessed for the benefit of everyone regardless of religion or colour. Now is the time for man to do something before it is too late, for wouldn't it be a shame if we had to find somewhere else in the universe to experience life because none existed on this planet?

The sad thing is that man can clearly see the precipice of his own making and with eyes wide open he walks towards the edge. Many argue that God would not allow such a situation to occur, but God has given you choice - how else are you going to learn? But it seems sad you should seek to destroy a planet in pursuance of choice.

There is nothing new in what we say, nothing that is not apparent to all sane thinkers but perhaps among some of you, the fact we have said it makes it a little more pertinent in your ears. We hope so. For those of you on the earthplane and us at all levels of awareness, part of your responsibility is to think of us as well - and that is something you seldom do. For all we can do is help give you choice, but it is you that choose.

The Mirror of Illusion

Once there was a great religious leader who walked our High Street of Life. He had time to spare between appointments so he turned into our little side street. And as he approached our little shop, curiosity got the better of him and he thought, "I must look inside". He opened the door and he had to bend low because of the low doorway, for no-one stands above the rest who enters our world, materially, they are all of the same level.

He entered the little shop. It was dim, and as his eyes became accustomed to the gloom he noticed the little man standing in the corner: he was frail and he wore humble clothes and nothing adorned him in the way of jewellery, but as he looked into his eyes, a great religious leader felt something move inside him, for there was love and compassion in those eyes and he felt at peace.

The clergyman asked if he may look around and the little man waved his hand with a welcoming gesture. And as you know, in our little shop there are rows of books, so he browsed through them slowly. Then all of a sudden, in a corner he saw a large package - it was nearly as tall as he was and it was covered in dust. He walked across. It was thin, just a bit wider than himself. With one finger he wiped the top and could just make out some lettering on the package: 'PART ONE IN OVERCOMING EGO.' it said.

He lifted up the package and carried it to the counter. "How much do you want for this?" he said to the little old man. "We have been waiting for you to collect it, sir," said the little old man with a smile, "there is no charge." "Will you have it delivered?" he said. "I'm afraid not," said the little old man, "for you must carry it with you."

By now the curiosity of the clergyman knew no bounds. He bade the little man goodbye and with the package, rushed from the shop. Into the High Street he ran and, hailing a taxi, was at his residence in a matter of minutes. He ran upstairs to his bedroom and closed the door behind him. With almost indecent haste he ripped the packaging to find out what was inside. It was a beautiful mirror. It was completely gold from top to bottom. "This must be priceless." he thought.

He stood in front of the mirror and suddenly the image of himself began to change. He was wearing an expensive-looking robe, jewelled from top to bottom and he was sat on a throne of gold in the most beautiful room, richly furnished, and around him were many lesser clergyman who were looking at him with reverence. He stood looking at the mirror for a few moments, wondering how it was that it didn't reflect his true self. And as he watched, along the top some writing came: "THE MIRROR OF ILLUSION' it said.

He gave a sigh. "It must be more than just an image of me." he thought. And then he looked down - he'd missed it as he had pulled the paper covering away – for there on the floor was a small packet, labelled 'MEDITATION'. He picked it up. He opened it and inside was a cloth. A little note fell out and he read 'THIS CLOTH IS IMPREGNATED WITH LOVE AND AWARENESS, ESPECIALLY DESIGNED TO CLEAN THE MIRROR'.

Immediately, he wiped the cloth across the face of the mirror and as he did so all the possessions in the picture disappeared. There he was, stood with his beautiful robe against a black background. He wiped the mirror again. Suddenly his robe of status had gone and there he stood, naked in the mirror. He rubbed the mirror again. And then slowly he saw himself disappearing like wax melting under heat - his identity had gone as well. He rubbed the mirror again. And suddenly it became transparent glass, he could look through it, and on the other side was a staircase. Then as he watched, an engraving came across the glass: 'BREAK THIS GLASS' it said 'TO ENTER THE STAIRCASE OF ENLIGHTENMENT'.

Suddenly our great leader felt a sense of loss. The stairs looked dirty and damp, and he had his position… "Was ego such an important thing?" he thought. "Perhaps if I stay this side of the glass I will become like the mirror of illusion." So he turned his back and walked away from the glass

He had exercised his choice.

Many will find it hard to understand why you should not be motivated by material ambitions. Say to them:
"We have riches within greater than anything you can offer us."
And so you shall have.

Chapter Three

Consider a ship: it sails from the port of birth on the sea of life and its destiny is the port of awareness. The ship's engines are powered by love. Sitting at the wheel of this vast ship is a high entity who has come to experience. His mind allows him choice as to the direction he steers the ship. Many thousands are on board and they too have been told of their destination. Around the sides of the ship are small life rafts and each one is labelled with messages of good intent so if the helmsman steers the wrong course, each and every one can get off the security of the ship. But the waters are rough on the sea of life and it takes a brave person to go overboard with one of the rafts if the ship should change to a wrong direction. But always there is choice.

So it is with war. No one had to stay on that ship, did they, heading for the port of destruction? Such is *group karma*. The helmsman was put there by all those on board so did they not then share in the wrong direction? It is the same in the world in which you live; you elect leaders from amongst you and therefore you must then share the responsibility for what they do. Think on that, for whereas it may seem fair in your eyes to abrogate responsibility for crimes committed under such circumstances, the truth is that all share some liability. Only those who choose the life-rafts are the truly enlightened ones, for no religion that represents a God of Love can justify any who follow it, for any reason, in killing another of their own. Such religions have been used as political tools by the power-seekers of the planet and even to this day many thousands die in pursuance of a belief against the basic understanding and teachings of Universal Love.

Always you try to abrogate responsibility to others.

Never accept anything on face value: always question, always seek the truth. Be sceptical but never block your mind, for through scepticism true knowledge grows, but with a blocked mind only karmic movement can change it.

Another thing that happens when you take on human form is that you frequently doubt the reality of your own thoughts and power. You aspire to give us the credit for your intuitive ideas when in reality they are your own desires and powers and manifestations, for are they not karmic, and is that not your role to play out? But with the opening to your inner awareness do you not see then the advantages of accepting the aspirations of the higher self, for it knows the needs of your body more than anyone. You doubt your own convictions, your knowledge and awareness, you attribute merits to others on a different plane, you assume that your higher self has no understandings or knowledge outside yourselves, you forget it is part of Creation and it is your mind's closest link to that source. So why does the mind seek to by-pass it? It is like trying to make a long-distance telephone call when a local one is all that is needed.

Let us return to the subject of transitional thought, for the understanding of this is particularly pertinent to karma and responsibility.

Your higher self is carried through life on a carriage. That carriage consists of all aspects of your being. Between lifetimes you depart from the carriage. The carriage has on top of it a roof rack that carries all the packages of karma from the past and when the higher self arrives and steps inside the carriage, the packages must be delivered on the journey through life to the correct destination. The horses that pull the carriage are the mind and whereas the higher self is aware of the destination the mind has choice, for the reins lie empty in the driver's seat. So we need awareness, don't we, to fill that seat and to pick up the reins and steer the mind in a positive direction. Karma may decide that the carriage must be driven over a cliff but if awareness is in the seat, it can pull the horses of the mind short of the edge.

Shall we call the carriage Transitional Thought, for it's moving, isn't it?

Sometimes the destination cannot be changed because of the karmic ruts that appear below, those that have been caused by others that came before you, but think on those.

We hope we haven't over-simplified what is a complex problem for you to understand. We try to present pieces of a jigsaw that will eventually build into a picture of the purpose of life. To concentrate on only one or two pieces would miss the whole.

In examining the law of karma we must also include the subject of reincarnation, for the two are tightly linked in the journey through the levels of love and awareness.

We have said that the road to awareness is through experience. It is therefore obvious that sufficient awareness cannot be gained through the experience of one lifetime only, one period in history, one gender, one mother and father, one nationality, one belief system, one occupation, and so on. For example, what of the infant that lives but a short time and dies of starvation? What of the rich woman that lives a life of selfish indulgence? It wouldn't make much sense if that were the only experience they ever needed to reach the point of enlightenment, would it?

The higher self has access to all knowledge. Awareness is what it seeks of that knowledge. What do we call the aspect of that knowledge that has been gained as a consequence of that awareness? *Wisdom.* It is that combination of knowledge and awareness that can then be used.

So the purpose of reincarnation is to climb the ladder of awareness and by so doing to become more knowledgeable and wiser until ultimately you reach level seven - the top of the ladder. And in the last transition through the last reincarnation you become aware of all knowledge and attain ultimate wisdom. The ancients called it enlightenment, the point at which we fuse with ultimate love, power, knowledge, wisdom: the terminology is not important.

To recap: in the beginning there was no awareness, only knowledge. Through reincarnation and the operation of the karmic laws, awareness is achieved and the higher self rises through the seven levels until in the end it is aware of all knowledge and returns to its source with all wisdom and understanding, thus completing the whole cycle of experience. You have then complete *love*.

So hatred and greed and the many vices and emotions existent in the human frame – the consequences of ignorance - are important in this process because they provide the challenges against which to progress and therefore understand the true meaning of love.

You take a little animal and you put him in the middle of a room and he loses his way, but if you show him a pathway he will follow it, won't he? Did that mean when you put that little animal on the floor that you wished to hurt it, did you have evil ambitions, did you wish to destroy it, kill it, make it experience a violent death? No, because you love it! But the little creature has freedom of choice, doesn't it, and as part of its learning it has to find the pathway across the room and avoid the obstacles. Those obstacles are always there, for they are the law of karma. Should the higher self not have put the little animal on the floor because the obstacles were there? It comes to the value you put on the human form, does it not? Have you thought of that? From the womb to the tomb is a pathway everyone must walk, no one is exempt, all must walk the pathway. The frame in which they walk is a temporary thing, one for experience and learning. Unfortunately, many see the frame as being all they have.

We have already touched on the dilemma that arises is in understanding why the higher selves of individuals should decide to perpetrate crimes on each other, for such is not the way of love and awareness. The experience of suffering is only part of the road of learning, like the obstacles on the floor. Do you not see that by being a law it absolves the higher self from the responsibility of that action, for it can be motivated by love and awareness only. If karma was not in existence that dilemma would remain, but if that law dictates a certain experience then the higher self is absolved from that responsibility, thus ensuring that it is motivated only by love. If it were otherwise then what would be the purpose of the karmic laws if the higher self already had an in-built system of its own? Then the higher self would reflect a god of judgement. Now you see why, when you throw overboard your beliefs in reincarnation and karma, you have to replace them with a god of judgement, with a god of anger and destruction. And what would be the point of a Universal Power creating this beautiful universe and then to go and destroy itself?

See as an example the foolishness of religious teachings and how they are being used in the world today, for no religion can be used as a justification for killing. The Universal Love of God is the same in you all, whatever the nationality. Yet one half is motivated by material ambition in one direction and one half by material ambition in another - and you seek to blame God for it! This religious corruption has got to stop! It matters not how you perceive God but only that you understand God for what God is.

Man has for too long remained under the cloak of misunderstanding. Let us all, using the steel of love, hone the knife of awareness and cut away the cloak of misunderstanding so that each may see the reality of love and understand its true nature.

How is karma experienced in the lives you lead? What are the most important points to consider?

Firstly, the interaction between individuals and groups: everything you do on an individual or group basis to each other in your thoughts and actions must surely affect your karma.

Secondly, the interaction between yourselves and the animal kingdom: the thoughts and actions that you show towards the others that share the planet with you, and their reaction to your thoughts and actions must also affect your karma.

Thirdly, the interaction between yourselves and the vegetable kingdom: the thoughts and actions you show towards all plant life of the planet must also affect your karma.

Fourthly, the interaction between yourselves and the mineral kingdom: the thoughts and actions you show towards the content of the planet must also affect your karma.

You wrongly assume that only you individuals interact with each other, when in reality everything on the planet has a part to play including the very planet itself. Do you see now how precious everything about you is? From the smallest insect under your foot to the very Earth itself, each is a manifestation of Universal Energy and Love inasmuch that from the rock to yourselves you are all part of the same energy.

You see therefore, the wisdom of being conscious of everything you see and do and of evaluating your actions and the consequences they may have. This is not difficult to understand, but very difficult to practise against the background of the material ambitions you set yourselves.

We have now introduced a broader understanding of the interaction of all things. What we have said is quite simple to understand; it is only man that builds complexities into these things. Why should he need to conjure these complexities in his mind: could it be because he has difficulty in comprehending the infinity of the universe, that he could not believe that it has just simple truths for its sole basis? A man today has no difficulty in understanding the complexity of a television set, but if he had shown such a simple tool to his forefathers, they would have gone quite mad, would they not? So as knowledge progresses, try and understand it from its simplicity and let not conjecture complicate it and at times even put it into the realms of fantasy.

No higher self exists within the mineral and plant worlds and their manifestation as energy moves within the level of *one*. Animals evolve through reincarnation, as Homo sapiens does, but move within earth-time at the levels of *one* and *two* only and therefore do not relate to the higher entity levels we have talked about. But the sensitivity and love in the universe is not the exclusive prerogative of you of the earthplane but applies to all creatures.

Animals do not relate to universal energy and understand its relevance as you do; unlike the sensitivity that was within all man from the time of his start. Many though, have lost that affinity through the world as it is today, but creatures still have it for they are less tarnished by the material world. That is why many prophets in their time had a great affinity for the creatures of the Earth, and throughout your history are many examples of this.

All animals evolve physically within their species, as your Charles Darwin proposed, but evolution also embraces the spiritual growth of awareness. Some of you try to assume that the animal kingdom is an earlier stage of man's evolution or even that man evolved through the mineral, plant and animal kingdoms, but this is not so. It was not until an advent of Homo sapiens' evolution, that the higher self moved from universal awareness and power for the experience of learning as we mean it within you now. Up to that point, man was the same as the rest of the animal kingdom.

That part within us called the higher self is part of God – Universal Love - and that part within an animal that relates on the lower planes is also part of God. When the increase in universal energy and awareness took place in Homo sapiens, it happened at the point of reincarnation, so nothing was taken away, only added to. It therefore follows that at that stage in its development, those Homo sapiens with a higher self co-existed with those still held within levels one and two. Their awareness would have been so low that it would not have mattered, but the opportunity of reaching higher levels as a consequence of the increased energy would have been there. So Homo sapiens at that period, the beginning of his existence, would not have been aware of any change externally. For example, when you look at a newborn baby, can you ascertain the level of its awareness? It is the same principle.

So you see how important a vehicle Homo sapiens is and how much better it would be in this so-called age of scientific and technological enlightenment, if he put his mind to the purpose for which he came instead of seeking the pathways of self-destruction.

We hope you are now more aware of the dire need for a change of direction in the society in which you live. We hope you can see the wisdom of what we say and how man uses religion in pursuance of political gain. We have no wish to negate the world's karma, and entities at our level will not predict the future, but perhaps wise minds can interpret the reasons for giving you these teachings and use them for world events as they occur, thus seeing the true spiritual pathway to take. If these teachings were available to all those at the moment who lead their peoples in religious and pseudo-religious dogma, would not the more aware minds amongst them see clearly what their leaders were at? They would not, would they, be able to develop and drill hatred against their fellow man for gain? Such has been the case throughout man's history because of the nature of the mind, the appeal of material gain and the insatiable desire for sensation. If we stooped to such measures there is little doubt that we would win all the support we need, but what useful purpose would that serve? For such would be direct interference in the choice of mankind, would it not?

We have spoken of the individual and the need for meditation to help the human race be more aware of what it does to the planet. By becoming more aware of your spiritual pathway you become more aware of the destruction of the planet. The two are not opposed but complementary, for what spiritually aware person could possibly hurt this beautiful planet and all the creatures that live on it? The process of learning is speeding up and man is becoming more aware but the time period is short, and always remember, the choice is yours. There will be no divine intervention to stop you ruining this beautiful planet, as many would have you believe: only by your increased awareness can it be stopped, for if divine intervention were the answer, then there would be no point in you being here.

Imagine a lonely man walking along a pathway. We seek to show him another path, one leading away from the material one he is walking, a way that leads directly to our bridge over the river. Such pathways have to be correctly made; they must be firm, with a brick construction. We supply you with those bricks; bricks of words, and you must choose whether to lay them in the direction of the bridge of awareness.

You have an expression in your world, "You leave the world the same as you came to it" and that is true of your material aspirations, for you can take none of them with you. But it is not true of your spiritual ones for you can leave this planet wealthier than anyone has ever dreamed of. Surely this is what life should be about - not seeking security in the collection of material things but of accumulating spiritual wealth. So what you have to gain is greater than any material possession you could ever wish for: awareness of the total knowledge within you.

The Tree of Meditation

When you see our words on paper, seek their meaning, seek to understand their true nature, seek to understand the experience of life in relation to those words. When you experience such knowledge, you then have mind-wisdom.

See the mind as a wood.

In that wood you have undergrowth. This is the undergrowth of emotion.

Also in the wood you have brushwood. This is the brushwood of sensation.

With the wise mind you cut away the undergrowth and the brushwood and then when you have cleared the ground of the mind you will see in the centre a lonely little tree. It is the tree of meditation.

With all the cover cleared from around it, with nothing to impede or stunt its growth, the tree will grow.

Seek not to force its growth, but allow it its freedom. For forced growth will cause the tree to be spindly and it will bend. Slow growth ensures that it is thick at the base and stout and strong.

And as it grows, this tree of meditation, it becomes the Tree of the Essence of Life itself.

We have talked of its branches before, so you know them well. We have told you not to look along them, but to climb to the top. This you can all do.

At the top is the higher self, so as you climb you come nearer to your reality and inner nature.

And while this process is happening within you, the mind becomes steadier and wiser and freer.

Sometimes you may see circulating clouds of fear around the base of the tree, but climb with trust and you can leave the clouds behind.

If you perceive others who appear less aware and you look at their wood of the mind and their little tree is suffocated, you can give them compassion and love and understanding. And if others misunderstand your motives do not blame them, for they have been educated in a material way and they see only the material pathways. But in time, by example, they may see your motivations and may understand.

All the trials of life are meaningless unless you learn from them.

Chapter Four

Why do you suffer pain? Because it provides the opportunity to examine the way, to examine everything and without it you wouldn't stop, you would carry on regardless. Through pain you question the reasons for your existence, you question your motives, you question your lifestyle, you question everything. And through that, you then form a deeper understanding of yourself. So it is an important step on the path of awareness; an experience you give yourself within the law of karma. The fact that the mind does not like to suffer creates the motivation to seek a meaning and a solution.

Therefore learn from the experiences and welcome them, for from the problems of life grows true wisdom. Always remember: the harder the lessons, the greater the opportunities for learning.

Let us assume that when you arrived on the earthplane and set yourselves a pathway ahead, if it was smooth in the material sense, if it was free of emotion and fear, if the doorway of your aspirations was thrown open with no problems, then what learning would that be to yourselves? So consider your emotions and study them well, for they may act as a pointer to your pathway.

Your energy is held together in the human frame with all its weaknesses and frailties and by overcoming the difficulties and tests you set yourselves, do you not see this brings true meaning to what you do? There is an assumption amongst many of you that your existence in human form should be over as soon as possible but we tell you this: savour every moment of experience, whether in love or fear or hurt, for such will raise your awareness.

You hold within yourself everything you need for good health, wise guidance and the ability to cope with any problem the world may offer you. However, when you first unscrew the cap of awareness and look inside with an untrained eye, it is difficult to distinguish between inner wisdom and imagination. This is another reason why the practise of meditation is central to living your life fully, for by creating a stillness of mind you begin to see things as they really are and not as the mind imagines them to be.

When we speak of 'awareness' in this context, we do not mean the everyday consciousness of the mind, for this is prejudiced by virtue of experience and the senses. In other words, the mind can never diagnose the truth for it is conditioned from the moment of birth to perceive each aspect of life in a certain way. The more stringent the conditioning, the more biased is the mind and the more it will react blindly from its programming. But as you train the mind through meditation, it becomes more detached and able to break from the grip of its conditioning.

The awareness of the higher self is another matter, however, for that is on a level beyond prejudice, emotion and judgement.

The mind draws constantly upon its conditioning to assess the importance of everything it encounters. Until you understand this, it is not possible to examine and deal with the motivations of your mind. Like the physical body, each mind differs in its genetic make-up and upbringing and is chosen by your higher self within the law of karma for the experience it provides. It is therefore no accident that you chose your mind, so love it too as an important part of your being but do not allow it to impede your spiritual progress. And if you have the kind of mind that opposes you in opening the door to your higher self, then the reward will be much greater when you finally succeed. When you see the mind in a detached way like this, when you truly do so, the door will fly open.

If the mind is not able to diagnose the truth then see the need to understand the difference between intellect and insight. The former is a conditioned evaluation of available information, whilst the latter is the intuitive wisdom of the higher self, uncontaminated by the mind.

Always you seek to satisfy the intellect, but *objectivity* is the key word to awareness, and awareness is the tool of insight.

You do not need high intellect to understand the secrets of the universe when you have an encyclopaedia of its contents within. This raises another important question, does it not - that of trust. If you have a deep trust within you that insight can provide the answers, then why should your mind doubt it? Could it be because you do not look at it objectively and therefore allow the conditioning of the mind to close the door? Simple to say, but hard to do!

On the subject of suffering, let us turn our attention to those on the planet that you consider to be disadvantaged because they are disabled in mind or body.

For example, what you call a mental handicap is used in a variety of ways to gain experience. Some originate from the law of karma, which the higher self is forced to concede, whilst others originate from the choices of the higher self for particular aspects of learning. Such experience can be gained from all levels of entity.

We have said that the objective of life is unity with the higher self. We have said that love is the motivator of life and awareness is its tool. So we give you an equation: love + awareness = movement. In considering those individuals with a mental handicap, the intellect is not part of the equation and love is there to be found within everyone. Therefore the only significant factor is the amount of awareness, and we cannot generalise on this because the degree is different in each person.

Because you cannot relate to the situation of someone whose brain does not function in the 'normal' way, you wrongly assume that the door to his or her higher self is closed. In reality the reverse may be true because they do not need to close the door on aspects of their mind that are not an active hindrance, like yours are. You attempt to understand your feelings and emotions in an endeavour to overcome the obstacles to your higher self but if these obstacles were not apparent within you, the pathway would be more open, would it not? Therefore when you meditate, you seek to achieve an understanding and awareness which some mentally handicapped people enjoy all the time.

You would accept, would you not, that without one or more of the normal senses, others are amplified? And the person without hearing has no hearing obstacles, the person without sight has no seeing obstacles, etc., so they are gifted, are they not? You relate all the time to what you consider to be the status quo, the 'normality' of man and anyone who does not meet your criteria, you feel is less fortunate. Now perhaps you can see the importance of helping disabled people to become aware that their spiritual pathway can be easier, not harder.

Consider the pure mind; it is one with its higher self for it has no distraction. Such is the babe in the womb, as we have said before. So looking at it differently, in a spiritual sense, you could consider yourself more handicapped than someone whose mind was less susceptible to the material world in which you live or who could not hear or see. Their feeling of love and spiritual need is always as great as yours - if not more - but because you cannot equate to their environment you sometimes underestimate their awareness.

This is equally true for those with psychiatric problems, whose minds may be in a constant state of turmoil and despair. Do not presume that such a handicap does not allow their higher selves to learn, even more than yours perhaps. Such cruel statements such as "Wouldn't they be better off dead?" completely misunderstand the role they need in order to play their karma through. Their experience is just as important as anyone else's.

So remember that mind-wisdom does not reflect the level of the entity within and that we are all equal within the love of the universe. Through many lifetimes we move through many experiences, so see not mind-wisdom as the objective of life.

The motivation of the majority of society of desire, hatred and ignorance has to be understood as the negativity within everyone. You should look at those three qualities within yourselves; from mild desire to greed, from mild annoyance to hatred, from slight unwillingness to ignorance: there is a sliding scale for each one. You have wisdom if you can recognise the negativities within yourself.

You help to generate love if you can seek to overcome those qualities within yourself. You have enlightenment when you succeed. Nothing has changed in the history of mankind in relation to those qualities for they have been embedded in you all since the conception of Homo sapiens. But if you understand the negativities then they can become powerful tools in understanding your awareness. For which one of you could admit that you have no mild desires, or that you have not felt slightly annoyed at someone's company? Have not the first two been as a consequence of the third - that we have not understood how our friend felt?

If you pick up the magazines that are now freely available on spiritual matters, and thumb through the pages, apply those qualities to the writers in each and you will see what we mean. All intellectualise, all wish to impress others with the magnitude of their knowledge - and on a mind level they nearly always do. But how many write of the true quality of love and awareness? And how many reading those articles would find them boring and uninteresting if they did? It is important to recognise the negative limitations of the mind for otherwise how can you go about overcoming them?

This brings us to another important subject: passive and active thought.

See the role of *passive thought* as thought that is produced by the intelligence of others. See the role of *active thought* as being that which is unique to yourself. See the centre of *no-thought* as being that produced by meditation - the link of intuitive wisdom within you, the key to the higher self. This is particularly pertinent to the present western materialistic society. When you understand the role of active thought, you then will move forward and develop within you a great understanding of the reality of existence.

So see our teachings not in a passive way, but see them as an instigator to greater active thought. When a child goes to school you teach him simple arithmetic: you question not why you teach him that, for you understand fully the reason you do it - so that he can make his way in life and utilise the simple information he has been given for the first advantage of himself. So what we offer you is the same. By taking these scribbles and understanding them, by using the activity of the mind in a new and unique way to you, you can build an understanding of reality, not just for yourself but for those around you as well.

When you turn inwards to seek the wisdom within, you need a clear understanding of what constitutes the mind in order not to confuse it with the higher self. To understand how an engine works you need to look at all the working parts and understand what each part does. So when you train a mechanic, if you were to miss out one of the working parts he would not be able to understand how the engine works, for each part is vital to its performance. Therefore as you progress in your practice of meditation, you need to learn all parts of the mind so that you can understand the true workings of its nature. Only then can you harness the power and use it in the proper way: to develop and understand insight.

One area of confusion is what is called the sub-conscious mind. The mind and the sub-conscious mind are one: they are not separate. The sub-conscious is that part of the mind that is aware of this lifetime only from the time of birth: it does not hold the record of previous lifetimes. So when your past-life therapists and regressionists talk of the sub-conscious with a view to looking at past lives, this cannot be done. Nearly always what these therapists investigate is the sub-conscious imagination of the individual, just like most of your dreams. There can be times, however, when the mind flies open and the higher self can break through, but like dreaming, the method is not reliable. So how is the seeker to know what is the sub-conscious imagination and what is the higher self, any more than you can know when you wake in the morning from a dream what is mind-imagination and what is your higher self?

Some people claim the ability to train their minds to access knowledge from the higher self in the sleep state, but again, this is not possible. Such contact has to be an aware process, aware of everything to a state of no-mind, which by its very nature requires a great deal of learning. This is not to say, however, that what you are trying to do in meditation may not happen spontaneously in certain parts of sleep, which is why it is important to listen to your dreams. But always there is uncertainty as to whether it is a higher self-related dream or an ordinary one and this is why you need meditation to help you distinguish between the two sources.

We have said that the central objective of life is union with the higher self. See this as your anchor pin, small and concise, which is central to your thoughts and actions. Then on the see-saw of life that pin will remain firm and from that you can raise your knowledge and awareness.

Have you ever tried washing a paintbrush that has filled with emulsion paint? You fill the bucket with clean water and you drop the brush in. You do this time and time again and the first few buckets are white and the bulk of the paint comes away quickly. Then as you go on the water becomes clearer and clearer but even the tiniest speck of paint causes the water to discolour. The further you go the harder it is to get out the last impurities but you still need the same volume of water. So it is with the mind: the further you go the harder it is to clean out those last impurities. But have confidence that what you do will eventually work and do not stop trying.

From the uncertainties of life comes a greater need for spiritual understanding.

Here is an exercise in overcoming the emotions and fears that so often cause turbulence of the mind during meditation.

Cleaning the Mind

If you had a house that you were proud of, would you not keep it clean of dust and dirt, would you not have regular sessions when you cleaned and polished it? But how often do you do this with your mind? So when you turn to meditation your mind is cluttered with all the thoughts and fears of the day's happenings and those which you think are likely to happen. Here is something personal and private that you can all try which may help you to clean the mind.

Sit down for a short period in the day or evening as if you were going to meditate but have with you a pencil and paper. Then as you sit quietly, jot down those private thoughts which come into your mind as they occur. That is a way of identifying the dust and dirt of the mind.
When you have done this for a while, pick up the duster of desire and look down the list of things and write by those things you consider to be desirous.

Then pick up the brush of fear and brush away the things from that paper that are motivations of fear and uncertainty.

Next pick up the dustpan of ignorance and see how many of those things are there because you have no information or you do not understand what has motivated you into an emotion.

When you have marked your list with these three things, see what else is left on the paper for it may be important. If there is nothing there, you have done very well. And as you do this exercise regularly, your house will become cleaner and brighter, for you will have swept from the corners of your minds the anxieties and uncertainties that may have been born of desire, fear or ignorance. Then you can control your meditation better, for you will quickly then identify the true nature of the thoughts that arise.

But please, always remember that it is only through discipline and dedication that real progress can be made.

It is time for us all now to move on, to see the real nature of the universe and how we are all part of it.

Chapter Five

The complexity that man makes of spirituality is bewildering. The creative force is so simple. Is it because it cannot be measured that we fabricate things in our minds which are not so?

As we have said before, in the beginning was energy: universal, cosmic, dynamic, energy. That was 15 thousand million years ago. As a consequence of universal energy came the birth of the universe. The universe, like all of us, has a cycle of existence and already half of that has passed. As a consequence of its evolution, planets of experience are born, such as the one you now stand on - and throughout the universe there are many. From the humble mineral beginnings of this planet, plant and animal life evolved and through evolution that life became more developed. As we have said, reincarnation of that animal life was on levels one and two and was bound to earth-time.

On these planets of experience, when certain animal life has developed to a sufficient level, these highly developed animals, such has Homo sapiens, become Beings of Universal Experience. By this we mean that the higher selves no longer rest with one particular planet in reincarnation, but move and experience as wide as the universe itself.

Are you now, I hope, beginning to understand the enormity of what we say and why at level three you leave behind all except love and awareness? Such beings are still within the law of karma, but karma operates not only on this but also on all planets, as it does throughout the universe. So the higher self chooses not only the time and circumstances of incarnation, but also the *planet* of experience.

This planet is young and Homo sapiens has only been here a few moments in the time of the universe. It is understandable therefore to realise that other planets may be - and are - much more evolved, supporting life with a higher awareness than exists here.

Let us look now at man. We have said that the level of awareness of the higher self gives you the wisdom within, but that you carry within you all knowledge - universal knowledge. That knowledge is not only restricted by your awareness in terms of the use you can make of it, but must also be restricted by the mind itself - and the mind is the main experience-maker of your life here. So you must therefore hold within you the very understandings of the universe itself. But your minds could not cope with such knowledge.

So if you have within you ultimate knowledge, that must contain all knowledge of technology and science. Let us look at philosophy as an example: if we go back to the days of your Isaac Newton, philosophy was within the ability of the individual and it was easy for the mind to accumulate the total availability of science at that time of your development. Such is not true today. A great mind now can spend a lifetime researching just one aspect, one minute part, of total scientific knowledge. Now you see the wisdom of reincarnation for it allows the experience of many lifetimes to be fed through for the experience of the higher self, and raises surely for analysis questions of how one individual in one lifetime can succeed in accumulating all the experience he or she needs.

So now man sees the great opportunities open to him, for you all really and truly are Children of the Universe. See your role not in sectarian interests, the narrowness of mind in the little world around you, for you truly are part of universal experience.

In the planets of experience, few seem to possess the qualities of Homo sapiens and his desire to destroy himself and the life around him. How can intelligent and hopefully civilised beings resort in a very short period of time to killing their fellow beings without compassion or love? On some of the planets of experience that have been going much longer than yours, two - or in one case three - beings of experience live in harmony with each other. But the evolutionary process would not allow another on this planet at the moment for you would surely destroy them, just as you are trying to destroy each other. Something for you to think on.

As an example, let us look at your dolphins: they are highly evolved mammals who in the future could well be beings of experience, whose higher selves might like perhaps to enjoy the levels higher than two. But that is only if you allow them to survive.

The time has come in your evolution to be responsible for less aware forms of life on your planet. Perhaps now you realise that you are just a part of the universe and not, as some of you think, the centre of it. Show more concern!

You are privileged with us to have a small insight into the totality of the universe.

As we have said, everything you perceive in the universe contains universal energy: the planet you stand on, the trees and plant life, the animal kingdom, right up to the beings of experience, from the very simplest life form to the most complex, from the littlest animal to your very selves. And as evolution allows the animal to progress, it has within it - each and every one of them - a portion of universal energy and love. We will call it the *inner self*. Then as the animal evolves, its brain grows in complexity and it begins to become motivated by love. The initial love may be very primitive by your concepts, may merely be motivated towards an understanding of reproductive functioning and survival - the very simplest form of love - but that animal also has within it a very low level of awareness. It evolves in earth-time and its reincarnations are held within earth-time and its levels are one and two. This we have told you before.

Many experiencing species of animals start to develop beyond survival, start to be motivated by greater concepts of love. Enter now *thought*.

Very minutely but gradually, the animal's brain encompasses a more complex pattern of working and gradually thought evolves. One day this thought reaches beyond survival and reproduction, towards spirituality - albeit in a very basic way - and at that point the thought becomes *transitional thought*, transcending time and space and linking to the very concepts of the universe and linking to the karmic laws. (The complexity of such arrangements must wait for later: we talk of only very basic points.)

That inner movement starts to formulate the inner personality, its energy increases and at the point of reincarnation that inner self becomes a higher self. And with the increase in energy comes ultimate knowledge and the animal becomes a Being of Experience.

The inner personality then becomes the vehicle of karmic movement and understanding. Transitional thought, which as we have said, transcends time and space, lays the foundation for that karma.

Nobody jumps up and grabs a poor unsuspecting animal and pins ultimate knowledge to it! It is all part of the evolutionary process of life, as natural as your progress to this present day. Perhaps you can also see now even more why your life is precious, for how are you to know how it will evolve and what shape it may take in a timeless universe? Realise how far Homo sapiens has strayed from the pathway of understanding.

A little more for you to understand but try not to get involved with detail at this stage: just take the broad principles and do not allow the intellect to analyse the information, for to do so would only cause confusion because of the limited knowledge we have imparted so far. When looking at these teachings, always consider the whole and not just one aspect. See how they relate to what you do each day and then understand your motivation. And if you feel these teachings close to your heart then perhaps that is because they are not new to you. You may know this intuitively but what is new is your mind in relation to these understandings, for perhaps this is the first time that the mind you now have has had an opportunity to consider them.

We've left a lot of points unanswered at the moment and that we know, but gradually now in your minds the structure should be taking shape. It is not difficult to understand, once you look at it objectively. That is why these teachings are important and that is why the ancient understandings of meditation are also important, for the latter prepares you for the former. You would not go out and buy a brand new suite of furniture and place it in an old barn, would you? You would find a nice room for it. The same is true of the words we have given you, for if you look at them objectively you will see that you can build a room in your mind and can encompass what we now say.

Seek to recognise the strength of the inner wisdom within you. See the mind as a coating and remove it and then you will have the strength you need to deal with your fears and emotions. And remember that you chose your mind to heighten your experience and by so doing realise true awareness. Cut away the unwholesome thoughts and needless fears and replace them with an inner clarity and tread the spiritual pathway of love.

The world economic troubles we talked of when we first came are beginning to happen. Let us hope that wisdom among the world leaders will prevail. Violence solves nothing, economic barriers solve nothing. You are part of a large human family and because the colour of your skin is different, because you speak a different language or have different customs, is that reason not to love each other? Look from the far corners of the universe to this little planet, as we do, and see how minute these differences are in a Universal Being motivated by Universal Love. Some of the early space travellers felt this. Homo sapiens is an important part of the experience but so is life itself, and when, oh when, will you see your role as part of the universe and not as separate points of power on this tiny planet? When will you truly see yourselves as Children of the Universe? When will your species move from the classroom and play its full role in developing universal experience?

This is an exercise in bringing to the conscious mind those emotions and experiences of the past which may be hindering your progress.

It is best accomplished in a relaxed state with the eyes closed, allowing any images to manifest without attempting to suppress or control or them.

The Attic of the Mind

Imagine that you occupy a little house, the place you have lived in all your life up to this point. Now, however, it is time to leave this little spiritual house and move on to the mansion of love and awareness. Before you move, though, you have to sort through your things and pack up only the belongings you need to take with you. The first place to start is at the top of your little house, in the attic of the mind.

Climb into your attic now and as you look around you will find an accumulation of experiences and emotions that have been there through your lifetime, some of them experiences of years ago. You had forgotten they were there and so you have to re-examine each one of them and find out whether they have a place in your new mansion.

There are some old cloaks of greed packed away in a trunk. Examine them and find your true needs.

In one corner of your attic sits a box of fear - you remember it since you were a child and you've never dared to look. Open it now and look inside, for there can be no room for fear in your new mansion.

In another corner, all dusty, you will find the books of enlightenment. You had heard about them but they looked awfully difficult to learn so you had left them. They are leather-bound with gold writing and as you open them you see that mainly they consist of meditation. Take them up, for they have a place in your new mansion.

Then most of all, there is a little silver box on the floor. It was given by an unknown relative when you were born but you had forgotten you had it. Pick it up and clean it and open it now. You know what is in it, you have known all along: it is the jewel of Love.

Do not be afraid to examine the contents of your attic or worry if it seems too full to deal with all at once, for you can always take a break and go back a later. And when you feel ready, climb back down from your attic and close the door gently behind you.

When you have cleared away all the old and outworn belongings from your attic, examine the furniture in the rest of the house and see if it will fit in your new home. Then when you move from your little house you will leave it empty and clean, and everything you take with you will have a place in your spiritual mansion.

*Seek an understanding of Love as you would of Eternal Life,
for if you have Love then you have Eternal Life.*

Chapter Six

We have talked before of love and awareness. We have said that love + awareness = motivation to the higher self. It seems simple and you would have thought it could be simply demonstrated by an inverted 'T', but instead we will use a triangle. We will look at this important subject and endeavour in a simple way to show the reasons.

Let us take a simple triangle with three equal sides.

At the top is the Higher Self, and at that point we will call it point 'A'.

On the left-hand side of the base you have Love, and that point we will call 'B'.

On the right-hand side of the base you have Awareness, we will call that point 'C'.

So we have a triangle with points A, B and C.

The line from C to A is the Line of Experience.

The line from A to B is Intuitive Wisdom.

The line from B to C is the Entity Level.

The flow of energy is demonstrated in an anti-clockwise direction. So the triangle is alive, it is *dynamic.*

Let us now extend the line AB and continue on a straight line down to point D.

Let us now look at the line AC and extend it in a straight line down to point E.

Let us now join point D to point E. We now have a larger triangle, don't we?

At point D is the Mind.

At point E is the Mind's Awareness.

The line D to E is the Line of Life, encompassing all suffering.

So we now have longer directional lines -

Line ABD now becomes the Line of Intuitive Wisdom.

Line ACE now becomes the Line of Experience.

And like the smaller triangle within, the larger triangle's energies travel in the same anti-clockwise direction.

Let us now look at what we have:

intuitive wisdom from the higher self passing through love - remember it is the motivating force - to the mind, the door-keeper.

When the mind is open - as it will become by life and suffering - its awareness is raised. The experience gained then travels up the other side of the triangle, encompassing the experience and awareness of the higher self and in turn becoming aware of the knowledge within, thus creating greater intuitive wisdom down the other side.

We have said the inner triangle is the inner personality.

The BC line is the Level of Entity that determines the speed of flow.

So we have a basic understanding of life and your role and your experience in a simple pictorial form, which you can all draw. What we endeavour to do is to reduce it to its simplest form, for it is easy to complicate things, is it not?

We will call the big triangle the TRIANGLE OF LIFE.

In our pictorial diagram the energy flows from awareness to the higher self, from the higher self to love, and from love to awareness, so it must therefore flow in an anti-clockwise direction. This is, however, only a diametric demonstration to show you how the energy flows. It need not be a triangle. In reality, it is the flow between the points that matters. One must raise the awareness to find the higher self. Love must be the motivator for awareness. So there is a loop of energy, it is true, but its anti-clockwise direction is only because that is how we have drawn it diametrically. Remember that we don't need clocks! We make it as easy as possible to understand and we think our diametric diagram explains it in its simplest way, and it does no harm to talk of triangles. But do not think each one of you has a triangle inside you!

You can see now how in our teachings we have emphasised the need to understand the workings of the mind. We have talked of mind-awareness and now you can see its role and how the little triangle can experience the aspects of life and why it is so important therefore to choose the right mind for its experience. For example, consider a highly evolved soul who has a highly developed intellect and an obstinate mind: such is no accident because the door will only fly open to allow the movement and experience of life to flow at the correct moment. You can also see now how the flow of energy within the higher self can still continue without life's experience.

The New Age, as you call it, has to be more than an understanding of the past; it has to be an understanding of your relationship to the universe. As we have said before, man has been here a very short time. It might seem a very long time in your eyes, but in terms of the universe it is very, very short.

Let us look at the mind and understand it a little more.

We have said that each time you reincarnate you choose your mind. It must be obvious therefore that each time you incarnate you have a new mind. So the mind dies with the body, and so does the large triangle.

It is true that you go from reincarnation to reincarnation to experience and become more aware of the knowledge within, but if the mind stayed the same each time you came then the experience would be extremely limited, would it not? But remember we have said that with each reincarnation you choose the mind, so you must be aware of its capabilities. The mind, however, if it is firmly implanted and looks along the line of life and suffering, sees no other way; it is ignorant of the wisdom that lies within.

We bring you teachings saying there is wisdom and love within you and that through meditation these can be found so the mind is no longer ignorant. But there must be something special in the mind itself, some energy that can open the door, a central motivating force of the mind. It could be referred to as an emotion. The word is *desire*.

Everything you seek in the material world is motivated by desire, and by overcoming ignorance you turn that desire inwards to love. It's as simple as that! So the quality the mind has for desire, if harnessed and used correctly, can bring about spiritual benefit. So within everyone, even to the deepest material-seeking atheist, there is a sense of desire, an *energy* of desire. So if you say, "I must meditate", you are turning that desire inwards; a desire for turning that desire inwards to seek spiritual awareness and love.

In the past many have wrongly concluded that the mind moved forward with the soul/higher self. But does a bodily function go forward? The mind is as much a part of the body as your head or your hand. The mind is a controlling factor in life but it is *not* your spiritual centre.

The problem emerges in the mind of man because you have not understood the independent nature of the higher self. The mind struggles continuously to hold onto its identity at all costs and your aspirations for its continuance beyond this lifetime is a reflection of that, for you cannot imagine your minds not to be immortal. But remember the lessons on the planets of experience, for we have never said that reincarnation had to be on this planet alone. Again, because of man's ego, he assumes there is none other. So the higher self needs to be independent, does it not?

So if the mind cannot survive death, you can see the value of transitional thought.

It is important to stop and take a fresh look at yourselves and begin to understand who you really are, to become aware of the entity within you. Your minds seek knowledge and they look to the four corners of the world for understandings. They listen to others, they read books and watch programmes, but you have all the knowledge within you right now. The only knowledge you should seek is to help the mind to cope with the realisation of who and what you really are.

You come to this planet to experience and we ask you to think on this: do you come to experience the knowledge outside yourself or the knowledge within you? And if you listen to others are you not then experiencing their knowledge? Look at the triangle and see that you experience your own knowledge and gain wisdom as a result. The writings of others can be important, but the only valid belief system must be what each one of you believes to be right.

Others recognise this and have done so for a long time. Examine the teachings of the great prophets through the ages and you will see how they recognise *love* as the main motivating force of the universe.

Anger and anguish, distress and hurt, are a first reaction to the way others are treating their fellow beings of experience and the planet itself but these are the emotions of the mind and body. Look upon love not as an emotion but as a motivating force, leading to true knowledge and understanding. If you give love unconditionally, then you open to the force of love from within and merely observe the results in an objective way. This is not uncaring or callous – quite the contrary – for it is the consequence of awareness, which allows action to emerge from a state of compassion without hindrance from conditioning.

The understanding of love needs to be central to all your spiritual development. We give you these five points of pure love to work on:

1. *Pure love is a love untarnished by anticipation.*
2. *Pure love is the highest manifestation of spiritual energy.*
3. *Pure love embraces everything.*
4. *Pure love understands the emotions of the body and of the mind.*
5. *Pure love accepts within its arms all hatred, anger, greed and ignorance.*

You see now why it is the motivating force of the universe. You see now why awareness of its true nature is so necessary.

When we came to you first, we told you of the famine that would happen at this time, with millions that starve. You now have a clearer understanding of the karma of them all but think of the perpetrator of their starvation, think of half the world enjoying more food than it can eat while children die. For we say to you that poverty and starvation are the worst forms of violence. And if you were to wage war as a nation and kill these helpless people, it is not much worse, is it, than when you have an abundance of food and watch them starve to death?

Ask yourself this: what kind of world would spend billions on high-technology weapons to destroy each other but would not buy a small bowl of rice for a starving child?

Throughout history many wise ones have shown concern and yet so little has changed. To solve the real problem, man must look inwards and understand the love within him.

When you turn your back on love you bar the flow of energy from within. Look to the triangle: the energy and love are unconditional but always there is choice, and when the world wages war it turns its back on love. If you lived in a little house as brothers and sisters and one was to kill the other, you would find such a thing inconceivable. But the family of man is no different. Does it hurt a Muslim to die less than a Christian or Jew, for are we not of the same family? And when your religious leaders talk of a just war to promote peace, we say to you that they speak with no authority but their own!

Many talk of a new age in which many will perish and believe that this is a divine wish. Nothing could be further from the truth. Such would fly in the face of our teachings when we talk of the energy of love, of beings of experience motivated by universal energy and love, when we talk of the higher self which has all knowledge but lacks experience. Do you think we would resort to cruelty and death to achieve that knowledge? That we would wipe millions off the face of the planet, creating the most terrible group karma, in order that the highly evolved ones could progress? Such thoughts are nonsense! It is man's greed and hatred and ignorance and *choice*. Cruelty has no part in our existence.

We understand that the magnitude of the world's suffering creates great emotion within some of you, but be objective. This is not turning your back. Be objective - otherwise how else do you avoid getting pulled into the fears of the mind if you do not adopt that attitude?

We say again that one of the problems today is that many of your religious leaders, in order to support their written words, have thrown aside the ancients' understanding of reincarnation and karma. Karma is a universal law, as we have always said, and if you do not accept karma, who then judges you, who makes you accountable for wrong deeds? And how do you say to the wrongdoers of the world 'you should not be doing this.' You have to turn universal love into a god of judgement: and that is what Christianity has done. For if you have a god of judgement, then he can justify killings, can he not? But they do not read their own teachings, do they? So now you see the value of karma, for it allows God to stand in the purest Love.

Where you have a god of judgement, the advocators of such a god can make a judgement on others and advocate violence saying 'This is in the name of God.' But if you have a God of Unconditional Love, you cannot ever justify causing suffering to others.

Such were the understandings of the original Christians. Where has their belief gone? Lost in dogma and doctrine, the invention of which is not of God, but of those who would use such interpretations for their own advantage. Such is true of many religions throughout the world. There is a need in all of them to return to the simplicity and truth. We have said 'You are children of the universe'. What happens to a little Chinese boy if he lives but a few months and dies without becoming a Christian? If he has no lifetimes of experience, no decision of choice, if his soul was born within this lifetime only - what happens to him? Christians never ask such questions, do they? Neither do Muslims. It is time to see past the futility and stupidity of such narrow-minded views to understand the importance of a Being of Experience on a Planet of Experience in a great Universe of Experience.

Broaden your minds to understand the enormous universe. Broaden your minds to encompass thoughts from other worlds. Broaden your minds to a *living* universe of which you all are just part. See then how sad we must feel when, in a tiny speck of that universe, sits a little planet, and in a small part of that, beings of experience are killing each other in the name of the universe. Do you see now what we mean by reality? How pitiful it all is!

Weld together these new understandings with ancient thoughts and help build a new society that encompasses our teachings in which you become true Children of the Universe with freedom of thought - and choice. And allow others to enjoy such freedom as you.

It is as if man will never learn, for all your leaders have mirrors of illusion. Send thoughts of love to the world, pray for peace. But when you do, differentiate between emotion and objectivity, for remember that your depth of emotion is not a measure of your love or spirituality but a consequence of the conditioned mind. If you look at it objectively, then the love flows from you, not as emotion, but as true compassion.

Learn love from the hatred of others.

We have said before that a God of Love has no place with war, but we understand that many people find the concept of pacifism hard when faced with the suffering of those who cannot defend themselves against the violence of others. Many wise and holy men have wrestled with this problem and 'holy wars' have been fought - but violence is never justified, whether by deprivation or war. There is, however, an important lesson to be learned from this dilemma, for the anger and hatred that can arise as a reaction to such situations provide the contrast for you to learn. Therefore recognise your thoughts and feelings and take strength in the knowledge that if you had chosen a mind that could have accepted pacifism readily, it would not have created this particular learning experience. Also see the wisdom of looking within, for if you rely on the mind it can deceive you. So when you have a violent thought, seek not to hide it and pretend it never existed but view it objectively and learn from the experience. Then you will see the thought not as an enemy but as a valuable instrument of experience.

How then, you may ask, does such a violent thought carried through time affect an individual? We say 'minimally' for it is the result of the thought that matters. If you suppress the thought, it will emerge again and again throughout this lifetime and then it becomes transitional to the point where it has to be resolved some other time. But if, by your objectivity, you resolve it then it is finished and you have no need for that thought again in another lifetime. So see now the value of everything you do.

THE TRIANGLE OF LIFE

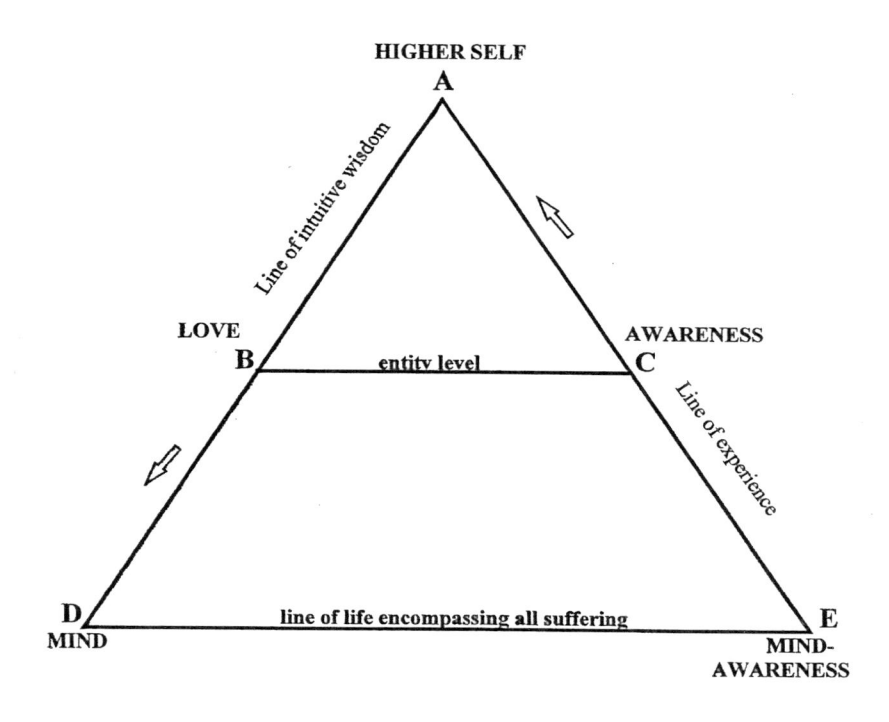

HIGHER SELF
A

Line of intuitive wisdom

LOVE
B — entity level — **C** **AWARENESS**

Line of experience

D — line of life encompassing all suffering — **E**
MIND   **MIND-AWARENESS**

Energy flows in an anti-clockwise direction ⇒

Everything throughout the universe, however small, has an effect on the universe. Everything: every thought, every movement.

Chapter Seven

The Law of Karma is universal: it applies throughout the universe. The reason we gave you a simple diagram of carriages and horses is because those are to be found on the earthplane. The packages they carry will therefore be applicable to the earthplane only. So a high-level entity arriving on planet Earth will incur the karma of a previous visit and that is why you have no knowledge of other planets of experience. Experiences vary from planet to planet and the higher your entity level, the broader the choice on planets of experience. The types of choice offered on this planet, the lessons to be learned, the pathways to be walked, are entirely different from other planets of experience, not only in time, but also in dimension. Therefore the karma will be entirely different as well.

Think for a moment of a high-level entity arriving on a planet that knew no hate, no anger, no greed, no desire, only love. Just imagine the choices open in such a widely different environment where the being of experience only enjoyed the motivation of love with no obstacles, with no hindrances between it and its higher self. Imagine experience with no fear of the future or the past. If such a planet exists for high-level entities then the karma created would be a lot different, would it not, to what you experience here? And the form you would take would bear no resemblance to Homo sapiens. This would be a planet for highly evolved ones.

We talked, did we not, of the Earth being young? Allowing for man's progress now, and assuming that the choices he made were a lot wiser than the ones he is making at the moment, what would this planet be like in half-a-million year's time? Would this Earth too be suitable for the experience of high ones?

Do your minds doubt the aspects of which we talk and if so, could that be the result of your conditioning? Such are the obstacles you have to overcome. But qualify trust with a healthy scepticism, for not to be sceptical would infer blind faith – and that is never healthy or proper.

One of the problems with the human body is that it is so secular, so sectarian in its outlook that it can see no other role it could play. Firstly, it has a problem identifying the higher self within it. Then it has difficulty accepting that it is part of the universe. And thirdly, it has trouble seeing the importance of the higher self and not just the body that surrounds it. Is it any wonder, therefore, that it is confused? We have spoken of this before, of how society seeks to preserve the body at all costs and ignores the Eternal Force within it.

When the nights are clear, look up at those stars above you and realise that you are part of them, as they are part of you. You are a microcosm of the whole, but you *are* the whole. We understand that this may appear contradictory at present but we hope that eventually it will become clear. Why should a small part of the whole be any less significant than the whole itself? Why should one small part of the whole be not the major part?

If you take a lorry and you fill it with sand, and if you take one grain of that sand from the lorry, it seems very insignificant doesn't it? But you are holding that grain and therefore it is more important to you than all the other grains, and its direction now bears no relation to the lorry. Therefore when the tipping mechanism begins and, for example, war is declared and the sand rushes from the lorry, you are no longer part of that flow. And when you look inside the lorry when it has finished its tipping, many grains have been left for they too have been held by the intuition within them. So remember this and do not allow yourselves to be tipped at the mercy of the lorry like the other grains of sand. For if at times your life does not unfold materially as you would wish, remember that if you are motivated by love then it will unfold spiritually as it should.

Motivation and needs are hard ones, aren't they? Whatever course you choose, you sometimes see them as a compromise. The greater your needs, the greater the compromises, and one bears a direct relationship to the other. So the less your needs are, the less are your compromises. This is a lesson few learn. Those who do learn it produce real happiness and true inner contentment with their lives. It is true that the conditioning of each individual plays an enormously important part in determining this, but until you are truly spiritually motivated you cannot set a firm base for your needs.

By recognising the conditioned nature of the mind and by becoming increasingly objective in your perception of life, you become more aware of your direction and the particular abilities you have brought with you. And when love pushes the awareness into active thought, then exhilaration, wonder, and serenity of mind can be experienced.

It's amazing what will happen when you start with a clean blackboard. And as you write on that clean blackboard with your new thoughts, do not be afraid if at first they look wrong, for such is the delicate balance between the mind and the intuition. You can always take a cloth and rub them out and start again.

The starting point could be the planet that you stand on, with your feet firmly planted on the ground, both physically and metaphorically, for then you join with the energy of the planet itself. For haven't we always said that the universe is alive? And so is the planet you stand on. If man saw it with its true vitality, if man saw it as a vessel of enormous love, would he abuse it so, treating it as an obsolete, inert object? This Earth is *alive,* we tell you, it pulsates with the energy of the universe. Such is the nature of a planet of experience.

You have about you an energy field; so does the Earth. Held within that field, within a lattice of energy, is the *karmic belt*. Such is the limit of level two. Understand therefore, the relationship to earth-time.

The cause and effect of your deeds is held within that karmic lattice. The lattice, of course, is held within a different level of understanding. A deed done now - a wrong or good deed - must therefore impress itself on that energy and be held for later adjustment. So the triangle of inner personality leaves its imprint on the karmic lattice and when it moves on to the higher levels of entity, that imprint within level two is the focal point for the transitional thoughts of that individual.

This is what distinguishes a planet of experience. The karmic lattice is therefore a reflection of the choices that exist within a planet.

Let us look some more at the reality of group karma.

We have told you that this planet is alive, that it pulsates with energy. We have told you of the karmic lattice. We have told you that the lattice is particular to this planet of experience. You can see therefore that it must be linked to the energy of the planet. The karmic range of each planet of experience is based against all living things upon the planet. So the anger and hatred you generate creates its impression on the karmic lattice as a whole. So we say to you, group karma is the interaction between the karmic lattice and the planet of experience.

Understand, therefore, that what you do to the planet today will determine what the planet will do to you tomorrow.

So group karma is expressed in the interaction of species and the environment as a whole. This is the reason why, when you destroy a species, you create an imbalance within the planet itself that is reflected in the way other species are then treated. By the end of this decade (2000 A.D.) a million species will have been wiped from the face of the planet. Such is the karma you create for yourselves, for even the tiniest insect is important to the balance of life and to the interaction between the karmic lattice and the planet. Now you see the wisdom of what we told you long ago, of the environmental problems that will face man. Now you understand the reasons why.

Through thought you can influence others in the way they treat the world, and through their actions you can then create *good* group karma for reincarnations to come. Now we hope you see and understand the delicate balance of life and how your love of the planet is so important.

Intuitively, most beings of experience on this planet, even those of a low level, have the awareness to know this is true but they allow their minds, for short-term material gain, to override the wisdom from within. Such is the nature of choice. You abuse the planet for the short-term gains of your material bodies to satisfy your emotional desires, and by so doing create your problems for the future. If you return to the foundation of love and give it unconditionally to everything you see then you hold back the cancer of greed that is growing within the karmic lattice as a consequence of your previous actions. Then by so doing you set about rectifying the imbalance.

As we speak to you now, the million is nearly there. Your scientists know this. How many, we wonder, through your evolution, have been denied becoming beings of experience?

As we have said before, any interaction of energy requires polarity within it: how else do you create balance? The positive and negative create the balance in the centre, just as your yang and yin. It is the balance between two points that creates the flow of energy. Spiritual energy is no different. The early theologians saw it as heaven and hell. You now are stepping forward to a new understanding; how one is essential to the other in the growth of experience and the development of wisdom.

Another question for you to consider is the difference between men and women and how this relates to spiritual awareness. Why do women seem to be more spiritually aware - is it a question of their polarity or of their upbringing from the time of birth and the way they are taught to live in the world? The higher self, and its level, is not concerned whether it is man or woman, except in the choosing of the vehicle of experience. Spiritually therefore, why should it choose a female or a male body? Many have indicated reasons for this through time but how many have paid attention to the considerations of the upbringing and how differently you treat men from women?

Men are taught to be aggressive; they play aggressive games and those who have great physical strength stand high amongst their fellows. This aggression also manifests itself in the material sense, and the acquiring of great wealth ensures the man has great status in society. Up until now in most parts of the world, the woman's role was seen to be different, but now she desires equality - not in the spiritual sense, for she has that already - but in a material and superficial way. She therefore seeks to emulate her male counterpart in his ambitions which run against spiritual awareness and needs of the higher self. Surely the reverse should be the case - that men should learn the love and wisdom of the women and become less aggressive and materialistic. This, however, requires a change in the values of society and that is something man should give consideration to. We should seek a liberation movement of men to emulate women, for they are the peacemakers of the world.

In the frantic search for knowledge we should never forget the motivation of love. The mind is a thirsty thing; it seeks to understand, it looks into every avenue of knowledge in an endeavour to understand its origin. So let us move on in pursuance of that knowledge, let us take another small step in understanding and let us look once more at our triangle of life and the triangle of inner personality.

In the triangle of inner personality let us find its centre: an equidistant point from A and B and from C. And in the centre of that triangle, we will call that point 'K'.

Let us draw a straight line from point K in the centre of the triangle of inner personality to point D on the triangle of life: the point of the mind.

Let us draw a straight line from point K to point E on the triangle of life: the point of mind-awareness.

Where the line KD dissects the line BC, we will call that point 'L'

And where the Line KE dissects the line BC, we will call that point 'M'.

The line KME is the line of Transitional Thought.

The line KLD is the line of Accountability.

Once again in our diagram, the energy flows in the large triangle KDE in an anti-clockwise direction and the energy flows in the little triangle KLM in an anti-clockwise direction.

The little triangle KLM is the TRIANGLE OF KARMA.

You note the base line of that triangle is the entity level line on the triangle ABC. You will also note that the little karmic triangle behaves independently to the higher self, as does the large triangle KDE.

What we give you here is important, for it is a pictorial illustration, a simple understanding, of how transitional thought can influence karma. Something more for you to work on.

Let us look again at the emergence of a being of experience on this planet. We have said that as the being becomes more aware, its thoughts seek an understanding greater than just reproduction and survival and at this point its thought becomes transitional in nature. That transitional thought then links with the very karmic lattice itself and the animal becomes a being of experience on levels one and two. The interaction between the planet's karmic lattice and the being of experience sets in motion the whole learning experience.

The creatures that share the planet with you do not create karmic accountability like you. You, however, can directly affect their opportunity for the future, for they are linked to the planet system as much as the trees and other plant life. Being animals they can, and do, reincarnate, but only within the two levels and with no karmic accountability on an individual basis. But as a group they too obviously must affect the environment of the planet. This can be worked in many ways, like the natural disasters, as you call them, which can directly affect the life cycle of many species. So you see now how interaction plays between the beings of experience, the karmic lattice, the planet, and the environment on the planet: all is a delicate balance. See now the need for man to understand what he does.

As you raise your awareness, you beings of experience, as you become more knowledgeable of the consequences of what you do, do you not see that you also become more *accountable*? So the entity line in the karmic triangle is very important. When you examine our illustration you will see now how the interaction starts to take place.

We ask you to consider what we say in context of all that is around you and remember that it only becomes wisdom when the knowledge is experienced. As we have said before, the words stay as words on paper until you turn them into instruments of experience.

But it is right to question, to accept nothing without questioning it, because only then will you realise the truth and it is a healthy sign, for anyone who believes blindly is not on the real path at all. The purpose and your presence here within this planet is to learn - that is why you came - so learn your lessons wisely.

THE TRIANGLE OF LIFE
TRANSITIONAL THOUGHT AND KARMA

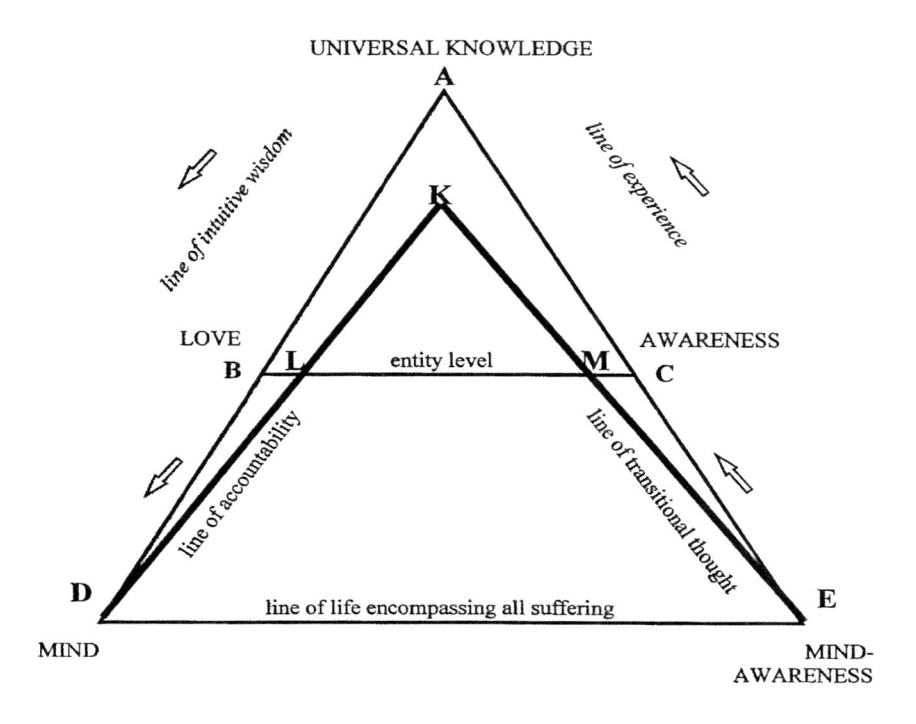

UNIVERSAL KNOWLEDGE
A

line of intuitive wisdom

line of experience

K

LOVE　　　　　　　　　　　　　　　AWARENESS
B　**L**　entity level　**M**　**C**

line of accountability

line of transitional thought

D　　line of life encompassing all suffering　　**E**

MIND　　　　　　　　　　　　　　　　　MIND-
　　　　　　　　　　　　　　　　　　AWARENESS

Energy flows in an anti-clockwise direction ⇨

103

*Life in the material form is a platform of learning:
the higher the platform, the harder it is to balance.*

Chapter Eight

If thought is all-powerful, why should you need to adorn yourself with gold and political power to impress others: why should you need to accept their values? For we tell you this: that the humblest individual on Earth can hold all knowledge and through his thoughts can change the world. The only thing stopping him is his own limitations - and those are of the mind.

Measure your success in spiritual profitability; that is all you need to do. As each situation arises, look at it objectively and apply that formula and you are unlikely to go wrong.

You seek to train the mind through meditation but the mind has expectations of its own. Therefore, one important factor to remember is that the only difference between a good meditation and a bad one is the judgement of the mind, for without the mind, every meditation would be a good one. So if you understand that, you can accept each meditation as being a good one. Then the only thing to cure is the judgement of the mind.

The higher self has no judgement, it seeks only to communicate: it seeks to give you its intuitive wisdom. But before it can reach mind-awareness it has to pass the mind - look at the triangle of life. See now the importance of training the mind, for when it no longer obstructs then mind-awareness is one with the higher self. For whereas love motivates awareness with the inner triangle, in the triangle of life the mind is the doorkeeper.

We have said that knowledge of past incarnations is not held within the mind but within the higher self. If you look along the line of accountability, as opposed to the line of intuitive wisdom, you will see what we mean. So if the mind is not an impediment to the flow of energy it must, within our triangles of understanding, allow awareness not only of intuitive wisdom, but that of the karmic past. But only in very exceptional circumstances is such knowledge of the past of benefit to the present time. For life is in the here and now: the present is as it is and the present is yesterday's future.

We have spoken of the healing exchange of love and energy so now let us explore an understanding, albeit a very basic one, so that we have a firm basis of knowledge to work on.

>   Let us consider again our Triangle of Life: ADE.
>   Let us extend our line AD to a point we shall call 'F'.
>   Let us extend our line AE to a point 'G'.
>   Let us join point F to point G.
>   Point F is the point of Object

Point G is the point of Object-Awareness.

Line DF is the line of Thought

Line FG is the line of Interaction.

Line EG is the line of Result.

So we now have a larger triangle again.

This is the TRIANGLE OF DYNAMIC ENERGY.

Line ADF carries dynamic energy, as also does line AEG, and all lines of energy flow in the same anti-clockwise direction in our diagram.

May we suggest that in order to understand the nature of the flow of energy, that you draw a line parallel to line ADF, slightly outside the triangle? That line we will call the Dynamic Energy Line. It is to illustrate that the flow of dynamic energy continues from the higher self to the object - to a limited degree regardless of the mind.

We suggest also that you illustrate the Dynamic Energy Return on the other side of the triangle on the line AEG with a similar parallel line outside the triangle.

So from the higher self a transmission of energy, motivated initially by a thought of the mind, travels to the object decided by the mind. Think of the word 'object' in a philosophical way: it may be a person, it may be a stone, it may be an animal, or it may be the Earth.

See now the basis of *spiritual healing* beginning to emerge. See now the need for understanding the mind.

The mind is the doorkeeper not only to your own awareness but also to your ability to share energy with others. Those who attempt to push the door open by ego will find that the true value of their energy will be small because, you see, the door opens *inwards*, not outwards, and the harder they push in a subjective way the less effective will be their energy. But once, through their awareness, they have turned the handle of the door, they can then stand back in an objective way and allow the door to swing open towards them.

The mind might consider that they are great healers but it is true that the greater their ego, the less is their healing ability. That is why many who just start as healers and who have a humble understanding, have great energy. But when others respond to that energy, then their minds often take over and no longer do they look at it objectively, for they start to quantify their energy and how the recipient responds. The reality is that if they are able to share their energy unconditionally then it is not for them to measure its success or failure because it is up to the object to take what it needs. And if they are truly objective, then every transmission of energy will be a success. This is so whether it appeals to the object or not, for the object's mind may be looking for the wrong result, that is, not what its higher self has determined but what the mind would like.

Conscious thought aids the transfer of energy but always remember it is within the recipient to absorb that energy and his higher self is the determining factor.

So through the Line of Thought, energy is directed to the object, and that still can then continue without the mind continually being aware of it. The *force* of the energy transmitted depends on both the entity level and the mind of the individual. So if the mind is closed, a limited energy can still be transmitted, but if the mind is open then the full power that the entity level permits can be attained. So once again we say, see how important is the training we have talked of.

So the Object receives the healer's power and this *interacts* with the Object's awareness. The Line of Result then responds to that awareness, enriching the sender's experience through their mind-awareness, and so through the line of accountability, sets the stage for their future.

We hope this basic understanding will help you to be more aware of what you do, for that Line of Thought can send energy throughout the world. The procedures are the same whether you are sending love that manifests itself in healing, in understanding, in compassion, or in knowledge.

If you are truly wise then you will use your power with humility and modesty and by so doing increase the strength beyond anything your minds can conceive. If you are foolish you will boast of your exploits, and you might impress others at mind level but nothing more, for as your ego increases so your power diminishes: one offsets the other in the total understanding. Always remember that the power is only as good as the one who gives it.

See our teachings now in relation to the religions of the world and see how many of their leaders fail to reach a true spiritual understanding because of what we say: *for the word means nothing unless it carries the love of the giver.*

Through your suffering and pain you have the opportunity to focus your minds on the reality of life and if you are wise then you will see such suffering only as a stepping stone to a better understanding.

Some of the ancient teachings considered that all suffering is a consequence of seeking, and within the broad understanding of seeking this is true, but the ancients did not understand the difference between positive and negative seeking. In seeking your higher self you do not incur suffering, but in seeking material gain - the opposite end of the spectrum - you most certainly do.

So in your search for knowledge you must learn to differentiate between those who walk the planet with material intent and those who walk with spiritual intent. There are many high ones on this planet but many of them have chosen with their minds to block their entity level, even though outwardly they seek to give others spiritual understanding. Look for the enlightened ones.

Would a truly enlightened one living in a poor country materialise trinkets for wealthy foreign visitors, or would a truly enlightened one materialise bread for the hungry around them?

Would a truly enlightened one accept the homage of all and adorn themselves in wealthy surroundings, or would a truly enlightened one seek the pathway to the poor, go amongst them and help them?

Would a truly enlightened one build great churches for the rich and powerful to come and join together, or would the truly enlightened one ask the wealthy to give all to the poor?

Pose such questions to yourself when judging the great ones on your planet, for a poor insignificant helper working in the third world is more enlightened than the heads of your churches who sit around and pay lip service to the needs of the poor. An outward expression of help is worth a thousand thoughts.

Look at your life; look constantly at your thoughts and the reasons for doing what you do. We have said this before and we feel we must say it again: if you are motivated by your minds alone then you set values of material things upon what you do. If you are motivated by the mind alone then ego is waiting in the wings. When you speak to others, look at the words you say and ask why you say them: is what you say to help them or to make them think more of you? If you follow these exercises then you too will become enlightened, you too will understand the true peace of spirituality.

The sad reality for everyone is that eventually you find no peace in material things.

Enlightenment is a true understanding of yourself, of your role in the world and the universe, the one-ness with Universal Love and Energy. Few have managed in the course of your history to reach such high demands. But remember that enlightenment has no status: no being is greater than another in the eyes of the universe.

The ancients did not have the benefit of the new age of awareness that is dawning throughout the world and they tried to express complex issues in a short phrase. For example, throughout its history Zen has sought to produce instant enlightenment but it has, unfortunately, only succeeded in those who have reached a peak of awareness already, perhaps even without realising it. So when you are sitting on the top of a ladder, the next step must be enlightenment, must it not? The concept of instant enlightenment decries all the lifetimes of learning it has taken you to get to that point.

Many have argued in the past that the ultimate sacrifice is to give your life for others, but to do so in a violent way, how can that achieve enlightenment with the intent to kill another? Do you think that would raise your awareness? Such would go against the teachings of Universal Love. But to give your life in love for another - that is a different matter. Understand therefore, that when you talk of conscience, you speak of a lifetime of conditioning, of other people's assessment of morals and values handed down to you by their prejudiced minds, for pure consciousness is awareness that is total objectivity. And with the coming of the new age, as you call it, such objectivity is essential in moving forward. So in everything you do, seek to understand yourselves.

Many on your planet fail to hold to their spiritual direction because they see it as separate from what they term 'living in the real world.' But we ask them this: what is the real world - a few thousand years of corruption and conditioning and suppression and violence, or millions of years of Universal Love and consciousness which ranges from one end of the universe to the other? Is it the prejudices that rest within a few beings of experience on a tiny planet, or is it Ultimate Knowledge and Total Objectivity?

It is time now to see the religions of the planet as merely a stepping-stone to higher understandings, for the new age must mean more than just the prejudices of the past. The child must now grow up and learn the responsibility of an adult - an adult of the universe, for we can no longer stand by and see them continue with their violent games. The need for experience is one thing but the continuation of selfishness and self-indulgence is quite another.

You have seen in recent wars the lessons of self-destruction, the lessons of man's greed. These are not the lessons of a god of judgement, but the consequence of man's inhumanity to man. The veneer of your civilisation, as you call it, is very thin. Within a short period of time you kill each other with no love in your hearts, only hatred. Such is the nature of the being of experience. Such great contrasts though, can lead to great awareness. They have done so in your history. Homo sapiens is young and inexperienced. The events we told you of have started, for the law of karma is an essential part of the universe, as we have said before, and what you do to each other now must surely affect your future.

With these simple words we aim to show the world that a choice exists. There are many sane thinkers on this planet at this moment in time who believe there is no hope for the world. But we tell them that if they follow this road it will have a steep hill of awareness to achieve but once they reach the summit the world can become a beautiful place. We say to you again, that those who purport that the only way this can be achieved is through self-destruction are quite wrong, for the world can stop now, at this moment in time, and take this roadway. "Why", you argue, 'should they listen to you?" and we say "Why not?" For there is no alternative to the destruction of the world until the peoples of the world join hands regardless of race of colour and live as one family with a common understanding to help each other. The violence will continue until this is achieved.

Most of you have lived lifetimes of other cultures, other races. Consider now that each time you come, must you take on the conditioning of that race, the prejudices of that race, the influenced consciousness of that race and the religious beliefs of that race? Why cannot you see your reincarnation in an objective way? For whether you are black, yellow or white, it is the body of your choice. So think carefully before you abuse another of a different race, for you might be that person next time. Think carefully before you hurt someone who is not as mentally aware as you, for that might be you next time.

Everything and everyone on this planet is precious. No one has the right to sit in judgement of another, for the law of karma will determine that.

THE TRIANGLE OF DYNAMIC ENERGY
THOUGHT AND INTERACTION

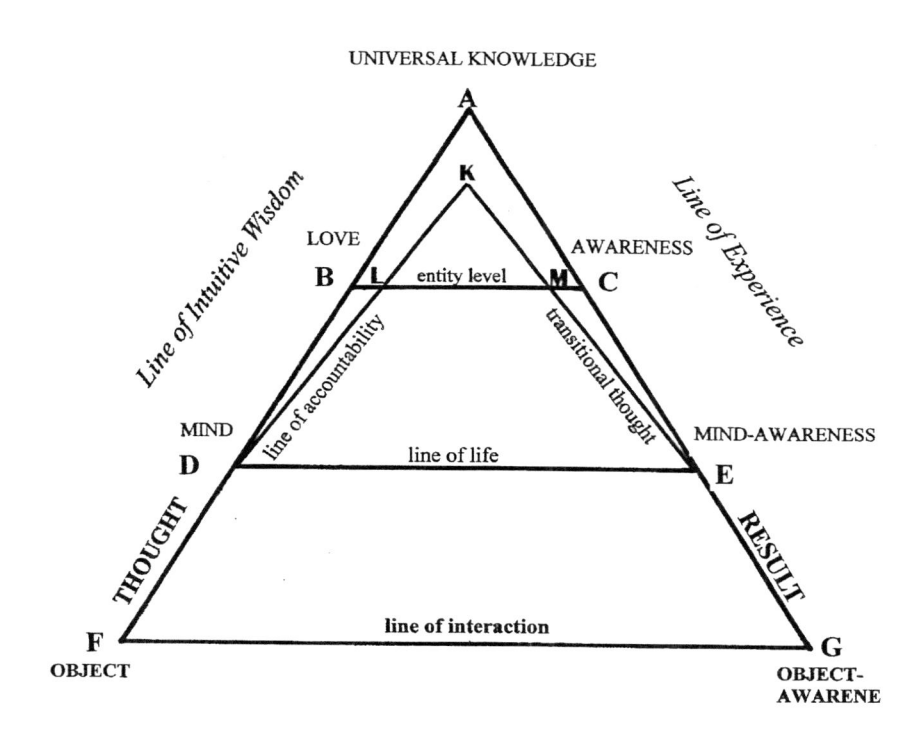

UNIVERSAL KNOWLEDGE

A

K

Line of Intuitive Wisdom   *Line of Experience*

LOVE   AWARENESS

B   L   entity level   M   C

line of accountability   transitional thought

MIND   MIND-AWARENESS
D   line of life   E

THOUGHT   RESULT

line of interaction
F   G
OBJECT   OBJECT-AWARENE

energy flows in an anti-clockwise direction ⇨

117

Man assumes he makes great discoveries but he does nothing of the sort: he merely becomes a bit more aware of what the Universe knew already.

Chapter Nine

As your scientists across the world look deep into the Universe in search of her secrets, it is important that greater spiritual understanding should go hand in hand with the huge strides in knowledge that are now being made. It is unfortunate that the same effort is not made for spiritual knowledge as it is within scientific studies, for you seek practical proof where no clear spiritual theory exists. For example, if someone from 2000 years ago were to view the universe through one of your telescopes of today he would develop the same spiritual conclusions as you do now because of the little progress you have made in this direction. The time has come to rectify this imbalance from both perspectives for as we have said before, science is that part of mysticism that can be measured.

There is a need for modern religions to interpret new scientific data and relate it to theological and philosophical thinking. Unfortunately, the narrow thinking of many religious leaders cause them to dismiss the scientific progress that has been made because it throws doubt on their religious beliefs, whereas they should instead be re-examining their beliefs in the light of current discoveries. As your new age dawns man should keep a balance between spiritual and scientific knowledge for they should not contradict each other.

Science is learning the secrets of life bit by bit. Truth in anything is limited to the knowledge you have acquired. Therefore as your knowledge grows so the truth changes, for the truth is only an assessment of the information you have available at that time in any field you wish to think of. Understand therefore, that it is difficult with your limited knowledge to comprehend the totality of existence but then, if you had ultimate knowledge there would be little purpose in pursuing your life.

When the first designer of the motor car put forward his ideas, did the human race visualise that this would be the ultimate? So it is with all ideas: they can be modified with increased learning. So through debate and discussion and understanding man increases his spiritual knowledge. Teachings such as these provide you with tools to build spiritual awareness and fashion a pathway of your own understanding and not just what we say. Then as you break away the rock and move down that path, it becomes smooth. You therefore learn by searching and feel more satisfied with the result if it is more of a consequence of your own thoughts.

We have stressed the need for understanding the nature of the mind and of dealing with its conditioned perception. We have advocated the practise of objectivity and meditation for this and as an act of self-enlightenment. We have talked of the flow of love and intuitive wisdom from the higher self and have seen the mind as a door, the controlling valve. Most seekers will initially look for their intuitive wisdom for its utilisation in their lives, for their personal development. The more spiritually able and dedicated amongst them may, however, go on to look beyond the mind to the intuitive wisdom of the universe itself. Those of a high entity level will then see the truth beyond the constrictions of this planet.

Let us return to our diagram to begin to examine the dimensional aspects of life.

A point exists beyond our Triangle of Dynamic Energy: it is the highest point, which we will call point 'H'. Point H will start well above point A.

Now let us draw a perpendicular line to divide our triangles in half. As it drops it will cut through points A and K, it will bisect line B-C right through the triangle, through the base of all the triangles to extend below the triangles to a point we will call point 'J'.

You now have the LINE OF ASCENDANCY for the triangle.

At the top of the line is point H, the highest point before you fuse with Universal Energy.

At the bottom of the line is point J, where you join the Line of Ascendancy.

From the point at J the line rises through the Seven Levels of Awareness.

When point H joins point A you have Enlightenment.

Let us look at the Line of Ascendancy, H-I-J.

Where the line crosses the B-C line is point 'I', the point of Intersection.

Where the line crosses the D-E line is point 'O', the Decision point through which the thoughts and actions of the individual directly affects their karma.

Where the line crosses the F-G line is point 'P', an important point, for clearly it can be seen that through your thoughts and actions to yourself and others you can directly affect not only your karma but also the karma of all things.

We now have three intersecting lines: point 'I', point 'O' and point 'P'.

See therefore the need to practice the higher standards of awareness in all you do. Examine all your motivations in life as an on-going process. Then the more you practice, the more of a habit they will become and the more they will occupy your life until you are aware of the very breath within you. Hard, but not impossible. And always there is choice.

Those who succeed will be those who understand the *true* meaning of love. Those who succeed will be those who can let go the material ambitions of life, for to try and take those values with you would make nonsense of all we have said.

Be aware that if you follow this path you will need broad shoulders, for you will be moving against the dogma and sectarian beliefs of others and the reluctance for change. And in making sacrifices of a material nature ask yourself this: would you prefer to emulate those rich and successful leaders of religion who have no spiritual understanding or direction? Would you rather follow those leaders who walk down the High Street of Life with their eyes firmly fixed on the windows of material content, stepping over the poor ones lying at their feet? We tell you that if you seek an understanding only of spiritual reality, then everything else will follow.

Let us look now at some important aspects of these teachings and at certain dangers that may occur.

Many will consider these words for their spiritual guidance, recognising intuitively that they strike a chord with their higher self. Some may throw to one side their old beliefs. But if we examine through the history of man, nearly always there has been a reliance on a father figure. Sometimes it has been human and sometimes it was necessary to create a supernatural image. There has been a feeling within man for centuries that he was not capable of finding his own enlightenment or salvation. This has been particularly true at times of high stress and illness with the need to feel a helping hand, a supernatural presence that could carry them forward. But enter now these teachings which carry a different message, which tell them all they need is within, which shows them meditation as the doorway to inner awareness and points the finger to themselves, saying 'You must find the pathway within yourself.' It is understandable therefore that suddenly great insecurity and spiritual loneliness may be felt. But those emotions are of the mind and not the higher self, for the higher self understands the true nature of existence.

However desperately someone may want to believe what we say, if they lack the dedication to meditate and find their higher self, they will find themselves spiritually lost, for as we have stressed before, the words are merely scribbles on paper until acted upon. The danger then is that the seeker may begin frantically trying to open more and more doors to other pathways in a search for satisfaction. And that is understandable, for what value does society put on the higher self anyway? The majority would not even admit to its existence and of the remaining minority, most of those would feel it has no role to play in their experience of life.

So if you feel the truth within our words, then see the need for showing those around you the advantages of them in the way you live. After all, when you buy a product in your material world, do you not normally ask the salesman if he has one? And if he said, 'I never use them' would you then buy one?

Always remember your spiritual aspirations: forget them not when the material problems tear at your heart, but put them into proportion against the total journey of your life and not just this lifetime and then they will not seem so important. The problem is, you see, that throughout your life on this planet the only tangible things you see with your eyes are material items and therefore they become predominant. But if you look within you will see the true riches you have within you: then you will realise the importance of the spiritual pathway.

More and more, the religions of the world are unable to cope with developing society. The narrow-minded dogma which most of them have encompassed over the centuries is unable to meet the challenges of the new century. These teachings will do this, but we do not expect them to correct in a short time what has taken many lifetimes of misunderstanding to reach.

We say again, let our wisdom be used with compassion and let it be motivated by love, for only then will it have meaning in the world.

May you choose wisely.
Walk with God, walk with universal love,
for they are one and the same.

THE TRIANGLE OF DYNAMIC ENERGY
THE LINE OF ASCENDANCY

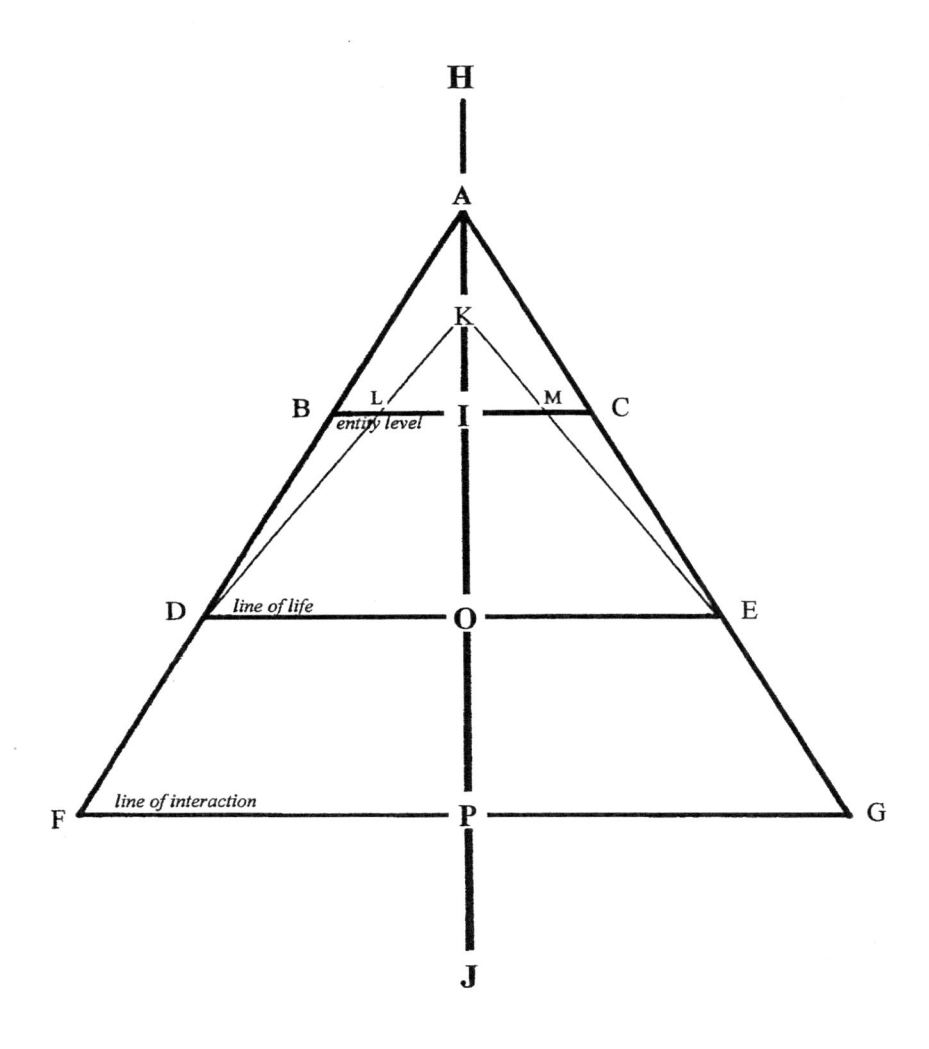

Perception of Truth

We are the voice - nothing more. The channel is the telephone - nothing more. The writer is the scribe - nothing more. And so it must continue, for you see, if you put a name to it, others will seek the knowledge of the name and not the content of what we say; then it becomes doctrine, then it becomes dogma. Each thing we say should be looked at for its content and not for its origin.

So my friends, what do we call the Truth? The truth is something you perceive with the limited knowledge you have.

Imagine a blind man who has been blind since birth. You take him to our Tree of Life and you place his hands on the bark and you say to him "This is the Teachings of Zed: describe them to me, blind man, tell me the shape of this Tree of Life." He would not give you a very good picture, but he would be telling you the truth. So it is with what we say. He would not see the branches or the leaves. He could hear them rustle with his intuition but no way could he comprehend the beauty of the whole thing. So all we can do is to show them the bark and then let each of them imagine the tree of life. For I say to you that once they have felt the bark through meditation, they can see the tree of life as it really is. Then no *discussion is necessary. But if you don't show them the tree they can't start, can they, because like the blind man, they will wander aimlessly through life bumping into the brick wall of religion and assuming that is the Tree.*

At the dawn of our teachings many will wish to join you to share our energy and love. Tell them:

Through perception you see the teachings and by so doing see the true roadway and understand the true nature of existence.

By picking up our teachings you knock on the doorway of your awareness.

By reading our teachings you open the doorway to the motivation of love within you.

By learning our teachings you learn of our awareness and love.

By practising our teachings you walk through life with universal love beside you.

So why do you need to see us when what you seek is all around you? Let it not be the sensationalism of our presence among you, let it only be our knowledge that you seek, for the love and energy that is here now is available to everyone by the raising of their awareness.

APPENDIX

A SIMPLE MEDITATION TECHNIQUE

The need for discovering the inward path through meditation is paramount throughout the Teachings of Zed. As they acknowledge, there is more than one way to meditate, and the aspects of understanding the mind and consciousness have been written about and practiced by many cultures for hundreds of years. For those new to meditation, though, they may seem rather daunting so here is a simple but effective technique that will provide the beginner with all the tools they need.

We need to begin by making a decision to meditate every day and sticking to it. As the Teachings say, the practice of meditation requires discipline and dedication. Without these, we will opt out whenever the mind becomes bored or distracted. Always remember that it's our choice whether we do it or not.

If possible, meditate at the same time every day. If we try to fit meditation in when we have a spare half-hour or so, it won't happen: there never will be a convenient time and we will reach the end the day saying, "I'll meditate tomorrow for sure." Then tomorrow will be the same, so give it priority.

Find a time when you will be relatively undisturbed. Early mornings are best because the mind is quieter. It's worth getting up a bit earlier. Meditating first thing also helps us to go into the day's routine in a more balanced state. Trying to meditate in the middle of the day can be difficult because the mind is already busy. Trying to meditate late in the day when the mind is tired is a sure way of falling asleep.

You might have to explain to others that what you're doing is important to you, whether they understand it or not, and always remember to turn off your cell phone before you start. If possible, choose a suitable place in the house that you can keep for your sittings with enough room to place a chair and a small table or shelf. The corner of a bedroom or study would be fine. The temperature needs to be warm but not over-warm and a light wrap kept for this purpose might be useful.

You need to allow at least 20 minutes for your session but 30 would be better and in time you will look forward to spending longer periods in meditation and contemplation.

Find a comfortable position where your body can be relaxed without becoming drowsy. A good position is to sit on a chair with your back supported and your feet flat on the floor. The spine needs to be relaxed but upright and the hands either with the back of one resting in the palm of the other or the backs of the hands relaxed in the lap. Sitting on a cushion or meditation stool may be more comfortable for some.

Always remember that in meditation the aim is to relax the body whilst bringing the mind to a state where it is awake but still, focussed and alert.

Now take a deep breath, close your eyes, and let go. Imagine that you are sitting in your own space, your own energy capsule. If you hear any noises, try to resist reacting to them. With practice they will still be there but will remain outside your 'box' and not disturb you.

Mentally check around your body to see if it's comfortable and relaxed. If you need to adjust your position, do it now. If you find an area that's tense or painful then imagine you're wrapping it gently in a bandage of light and it will feel easier.

Take a few more deep breaths and imagine you're drawing your breath in from across the universe and filling every part of your body, right down into the abdomen. Then as you breathe out, imagine you're breathing out tension and anxiety. After a little while allow your breathing to settle to a natural rhythm.

Now bring your attention gently to the breath moving in and out of your body. Notice how, when you breathe in, your abdomen rises, and when you breathe out, it falls. Lightly observe this rise and fall of the abdomen.

When you realise that your mind has wandered off, don't get cross, don't indulge the thought and follow it, and don't try and suppress it either. Instead, put a screen up in front of your closed eyes, put the thought on the screen and see how it arose, how it got there. Then let it slide off the screen and go back to the gentle awareness of the breath and the rise and fall of the abdomen. Do this again and again.

Eventually the mind will become quieter, but be aware this doesn't happen to order.

If colours or images come up on your screen, simply observe them as if you were at the cinema and don't indulge them. Be the observer, not the projectionist. Let them pass. Some people see these images and others don't. They are not an indication of achievement. Psychic awareness has a role to play but meditation is the key to its development by mastering the mind.

You will probably find that you come out of your meditation at exactly the time you planned. Have a good stretch, plant your feet firmly on the floor, take a couple of deep breaths and then get on with your day with the intention of being as mindful as you can.

The most important thing to remember is that meditation is a *process*, it is not some therapy that produces instant results, so make a pact with yourself to sit every day, even when your mind is trying to persuade you otherwise.

Each time you sit it is likely to be different so having an expectation of what you want from it will most likely lead to disappointment. Just sitting and dealing with the mind is the most important thing of all. It will change your life.

JT

*For additional copies of this book
or general enquiries please go to
www.worldawarenesstrust.org*